D0759778

784.028
A232c

CHORAL ARRANGING

BY

HAWLEY ADES

Shawnee Press, Inc.
Delaware Water Gap, Pa.

66236

Copyright © 1966 by Shawnee Press, Inc.
International Copyright Secured All rights reserved
Printed in U. S. A.
First edition

Library of Congress Catalog Card No. 66-26278
(M-224)

PREFACE

THIS book is written for the choral arranger of today — director, student, or composer. Its purpose is to present an organized program of study for musicians interested in writing for voices.

Both my work as a choral arranger for professional and amateur groups and my experience teaching choral arranging have pointed to the need for such a book. Though there are a number of comprehensive texts available to the student of orchestration, there is not a comparable work dealing with writing for voices. While the term "choral arranging" can be applied to any vocal writing from simple harmonization of a melody to vocal settings so creative that they are really composition, this book deals with the range of writing between these extremes — that is, practical choral arranging for the musician who wishes to make an effective setting of a particular piece of musical material for a particular choral group.

The composer too may find this presentation of choral arranging of value in indicating possible means of setting his original musical ideas, though the choral arranger, of course, looks to the composer to expand these techniques. In fact, because all of our present choral arranging techniques stem from great choral compositions of the past, many of the examples used in this book are drawn from original works. In connection with this use of examples from original compositions, I should explain that when reference is made to various devices and techniques in these illustrations as "arranging" devices, this is to point these out and add them to the choral arranger's musical vocabulary. My purpose is to help the choral arranger develop an effective skill rather than to ascertain whether a given device or technique should be termed "arranging" or "composing". That is, this book is intended as a practical handbook on the subject of choral writing rather than as an academic exploration of it.

As prerequisites to taking up this study of choral arranging, I assume the student's working knowledge of harmony and counterpoint. In addition, he should have a sufficient background in music history to provide a grasp of the distinguishing characteristics of various styles and periods of composition, for stylistic consistency is the main hallmark of the skilled arranger. Such a knowledge enables the arranger to choose and maintain an appropriate style for a given setting, using contrapuntal devices from the Baroque period, nineteenth-century chromaticism, or the harmonic and rhythmic idioms of the twentieth century, as indicated by the character of the musical material.

Also needed is a background of association with singers and singing groups, and of greatest value is a current affiliation with a choral group which provides opportunity to hear one's writing. A thorough knowledge of the capabilities and limitations of voices cannot be acquired except by working with a singing group. Though the general classification and ranges of voices are easily mastered, there are many subtleties of timbre, tessitura, vocal line, and dynamic balance between sections and an infinite variety of tone coloration and dramatic expression which must be heard many times over to be handled with assurance.

In this book are a number of new terms, special references, and other personal usages. I make no excuse for coining phrases such as "choral cadenza", nor do I attempt to explain general terms, such as "serious music", as these will be understood within the context of the book. If examples by George Frederick Handel and Hoagy Carmichael are useful in illustrating a particular point, I believe the proximity of these two composers is justified.

At the end of each chapter are suggestions for further reference and study. In addition, the appendix contains a bibliography of supplementary examples. Together, these comprise material for practice assignments to be used as a guide by the teacher and student. The completion of these supplementary studies is highly recommended for anyone undertaking the mastery of choral arranging. Use of these supplementary lessons is particularly valuable in classes where such material can be the basis for more extensive projects.

I was unable to include one chapter I had originally intended to make part of this book — namely, a discussion of the copyright law as it pertains to the arranger. I could not include this information because the U.S. Congress is in the process of considering a revised copyright law and its provisions will not be known for some time. However, I would caution the arranger to show careful respect for the property rights claimed by the copyright notice on any piece of music and not to make any copy of any work without permission from the copyright owner or positive knowledge that the work is in the public domain. For complete information on the copyright law, write to Superintendent of Documents, Government Printing Office, Washington, D. C. For a brief and less technical summary of the law as it applies to music, write for "copyright pamphlet" from the Music Publishers Association, 609 Fifth Avenue, New York, New York.

Acknowledgment is gratefully made to a great many publishers for granting permission to include examples from copyrighted works. Through such cooperation we have been able to provide a generous number of examples to illustrate points under discussion.

Also, I wish to express my appreciation to all those who have assisted me in the preparation of this book. I am particularly grateful to Tibor Serly, Helmy Kresa, Buddy DuFault, Lara Hoggard, and Livingston Gearhart for advice and technical assistance, to Dr. Paul Van Bodegraven for the opportunity to experiment with the text at New York University under actual teaching conditions, to Robert Olson for his very substantial contribution to the reference and study suggestions, and to Jean Ann Wolbert and Marjorie Farmer for help in preparing the manuscript and proof-reading. Most importantly, I want to thank Fred Waring for providing me with the opportunity to learn choral arranging. During a period of more than twenty years, writing for the Waring Glee Club has furnished the most gratifying learning situation and challenging testing ground for ideas that an arranger can have. Indeed, if the choral arranger is to learn his craft, there is no substitute for writing and hearing, then writing again.

H. A.

CONTENTS

CHAPTER 1

PRINCIPLES OF PART WRITING FOR VOICES

THE basic principles of good part writing are essential tools for the choral arranger. Although these principles are, in varying degrees, also applicable to two-part, three-part and multiple-part writing, in this first chapter they will be considered in the most traditional voicing for chorus — four-part writing.

Vocal ranges

Ranges for the respective voices of the mixed chorus are shown below. White notes show the normal ranges for most non-professional groups; black notes represent extensions of these ranges for exceptional and professional choruses. The latter should be employed sparingly even under the most favorable circumstances and reserved for short climactic fortissimo passages or for special effects. These passages must be short because prolonged singing in extremely high or low tessitura will overtax the voices.

In writing unison passages for either beginning or advanced groups, limited use of the extended ranges is permissible in the downward extension for Soprano and Tenor and the upward extension for Alto and Bass, provided these voices need not strain to maintain volume but can rely on the sections still in normal ranges.

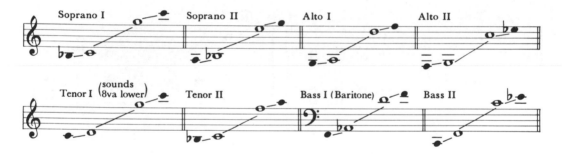

Discussion of ranges for special groups of voices will be found in sections dealing with those groupings.

Melodic voice parts

The fundamental law of good part writing requires that each part move smoothly and melodically. Corollaries to this law are that, (1) diatonic (stepwise) movement and leaps of a third are always good.

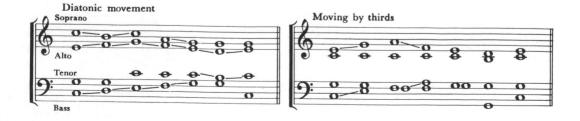

(2) leaps greater than a third are more difficult and must be handled with greater care. Rules which apply are:

a) After a wide leap, a melodic line usually changes direction, as in Ⓐ, but may continue in the same direction when moving within the same chord, as in Ⓑ.

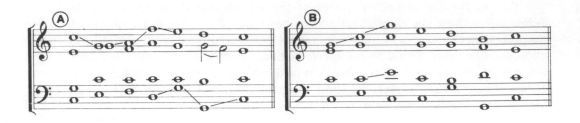

b) The melodic line may likewise continue in the same direction if the movement following the leap is diatonic (See Ⓐ), or if the tone to which the wide leap is made is sustained long enough to imply a new melodic starting point, as in Ⓑ.

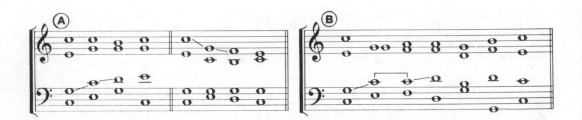

Difficult intervals

Certain intervals are quite difficult to sing and should be avoided, particularly when writing for inexperienced groups. The most hazardous intervals are augmented seconds and augmented fourths upward, and diminished fifths downward.

An exception to this rule occurs when voices merely shift position within the same chord, in which case, these intervals are readily heard because another voice will be sounding the note to which a leap must be made.

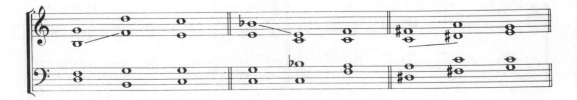

Some of the difficulties arising from the use of augmented seconds may be resolved through judicious voice leading. Observe that smooth voice leading in Ⓑ required doubling the third in a tonic chord. In such situations good voice leading usually takes precedence over the traditionally recommended doubling within isolated chord structures.

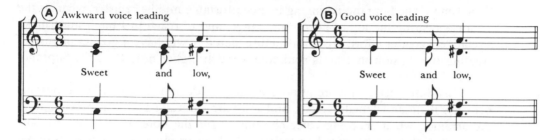

When alteration of voice leading is impractical, enharmonic spelling may be used. In Ⓐ, the augmented second from C to D sharp is difficult to hear and sing. In Ⓑ, the same interval spelled enharmonically becomes a minor 3rd, C to E flat, and is now easy to sing.

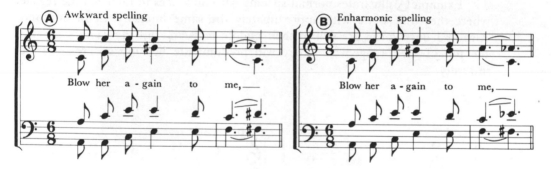

Close voicing and open voicing

Close voicing is spacing vocal parts with the three upper voices within an octave, as in Ⓐ. Open voicing is spacing the voice parts with the upper three voices spanning an interval greater than an octave, as in Ⓑ.

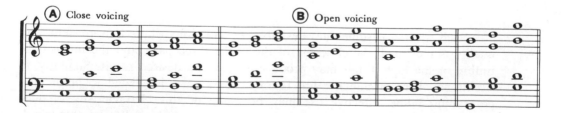

Because continued use of either closed or open voicing tends to result in stylistic monotony, free interchange between the two is recommended, except when a monochrome effect is desired. (See Exs. 12, 13, 14.)

Male and treble voice intensity

The difference in the relative intensity of the same note as sung by male and treble voices frequently confuses the inexperienced arranger. The problem can perhaps best be visualized by considering the difference in tonal timbre which results from the mezzo-forte sounding of the G above Middle C by a Soprano and by a Tenor. The Soprano is singing in a comfortable middle register, whereas the Tenor is nearing the top of his normal range, and to reach this pitch must make a relatively greater effort. His vocal timbre therefore will have a greater intensity, creating the illusion that he is sounding a much higher note than the Soprano.

This difference in timbre applies in varying degrees to all the relationships between male and female voices, and must be carefully taken into account by the arranger when choosing voice placements for the notes in each chord. The basic principle may be stated as follows: Any given pitch will appear to sound higher when sung by a male voice than will the same pitch sung by a treble voice.

Example Ⓐ illustrates normal spacing with all voices in their middle register where they will sound with approximately the same intensity. In Ⓑ, Soprano, Alto and Bass voices are still in their middle registers, but the Tenors are near the top of their range where they will predominate because of greater vocal intensity.

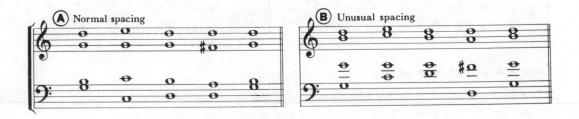

Such spacing is sometimes desirable. In situations where a more stentorian quality is indicated, the closeness of the upper three parts and the intensity of timbre of the high Tenor may produce exactly the desired result. Similarly, in situations where prominence for Tenor or Bass parts is needed to point up a contrapuntal line, effective use may be made of this characteristic of male voices. In order to observe the operation of this principle and to be able to calculate carefully the effect of any variation from normal range relationships, the student should hear the above examples as well as others. A few moments of careful listening will prove more instructive than many paragraphs of explanation.

Limits of intervals between voices

The general rule for spacing vocal parts is that no two adjacent parts should be separated by more than an octave. Greater intervals may occasionally be permitted if they are not long continued and if needed to achieve smooth voice leading. The use of larger intervals between Tenor and Bass voices is more common than between Tenor and Alto or Alto and Soprano. This rule, as with others applying to part writing, defines generally advisable procedure, and may be disregarded when the musical circumstances require an unusual treatment. The general rule is illustrated in the following examples.

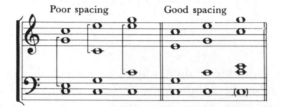

Doublings

The doubling of notes in all triads is governed by the basic principle that the best tones to double are the principal steps of the scale, the tonic, dominant and subdominant. From this principle follows the rule that in the principal triads, I, IV and V, the root is doubled when these chords appear in root position, while in inversions either the root or the fifth may be doubled. The corollary to this rule prohibits the doubling of the third, particularly when these chords are used in first inversion, with the third in the bass. Since it is the first inversion which is most apt to be troublesome, we illustrate doublings within the tonic chord in that position. These also apply to the dominant and subdominant chords.

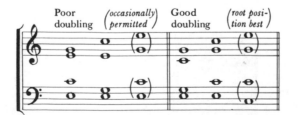

From the principle that the best tones to double are the principal steps of the scale, the tonic, dominant and subdominant, we derive also the rule that the third is the best tone to double in the subordinate triads, II, III, and VI. The roots of these chords may also be doubled because of their harmonic importance to these structures; in inversions the fifth may be doubled. We illustrate doublings in the II chord in first inversion in the following example. Similar doublings apply to the III and VI chords.

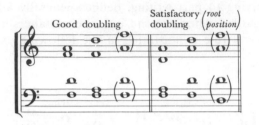

The foregoing rules for doublings apply in general to both major and minor triads. The outstanding exception is the II chord in minor keys, which is a diminished triad and therefore requires inversion. First inversion is best with either root or, more commonly, the third being doubled. The following examples illustrate correct and incorrect doublings.

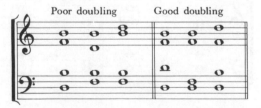

The triad on the seventh step of the scale, the leading tone, is infrequently used. Again, as a diminished triad it requires inversion, first inversion being best with anything doubled except the leading tone.

In dominant seventh chords in root position, the fifth may be omitted and the root doubled. Unless the melodic line necessitates this, it is just as well to include all four tones of the chord.

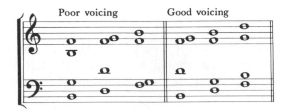

In inversions of the dominant seventh chords, all four tones must be included.

All rules for doublings in dominant seventh chords apply equally to secondary sevenths, diminished chords, and augmented sixth chords. In the latter, it is usually inadvisable to use inversions which do not permit inclusion of the interval of the augmented sixth.

In dominant ninth chords in root position the least important of the five tones, the fifth, is omitted.

In all inversions of dominant ninth chords the root is omitted. In major keys the ninth must not appear in the bass in traditional harmonization.

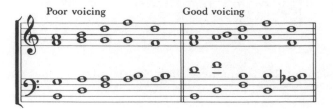

Rules for doubling of parts apply only to traditional choral writing in which the bass voices carry the fundamental bass line of the harmonic structure. In other types of writing, particularly those using parallel motion, they may be disregarded.

Chord progression in traditional style

Common tones

A tone common to two consecutive chords should usually be retained in the same voice as in Ⓐ, though occasional exceptions will occur as in Ⓑ and Ⓒ. In the latter, the G is a common tone not retained in the same voice.

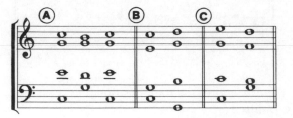

Tonal tendencies

The leading tone, the seventh step of the scale, has a strong tendency to resolve upward, and this tendency should usually be respected. Occasionally a downward leap of a third to the dominant is permitted in an inner part to attain complete harmonization of the tonic chord. This liberty is more common in close voicing where the inner parts are heard less prominently.

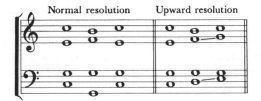

In dominant seventh chords the normal resolution of the seventh is downward, but occasional upward resolution is permitted when the seventh ascends diatonically in thirds or tenths with the bass.

Consecutive fifths and octaves

The traditional prohibition against consecutive fifths and octaves is soundly based upon the principle that they reduce the number of independent vocal lines and tend to create an effect of stiffness and rigidity. The prohibition still applies in traditional four-part work and is a valuable means of achieving smooth part writing.

In current usage many composers disregard this prohibition, particularly when they desire an effect of rugged strength which may actually be enhanced by the stiffness and rigidity of parallel fifths and octaves. The following two examples illustrate this usage in modern writing. The student should be cautioned to use parallel fifths and octaves only when he is sure their effect is desired.

Ex. 1   "Song of the Open Road" — N. Dello Joio
© Copyright MCMLIII, Carl Fischer, Inc.

Ex. 2 "Songs of Conquest" — H. McDonald
Ⓒ Copyright MCMXXXVII, MCMXXXIX, Elkan-Vogel Co., Inc. - Elkan-Vogel Co., copyright owners, Philadelphia, Pa.

Contrary motion

Good traditional part writing requires the use of contrary motion in one or more parts whenever possible. As a corollary, when contrary motion is impractical, one or more parts should retain the tones common to consecutive chords. These procedures impart to the writing that sense of balance and solidity which is characteristic of the traditional style illustrated in Ex. 3.

Ex. 3 "Jesus Christ Is Ris'n Today"

A number of exceptions to the preceding rules will be noted throughout this volume in treating musical materials suggesting emphasis on buoyancy and movement. In such instances, parallel motion in all parts is recommended. One such situation is illustrated in the following example, which shows the surging effect of an upward and downward sweep in parallel motion.

Ex. 4

Repeated notes

To avoid the stiff, static quality resulting from reiteration of the same note, particularly in inner parts, simply interchange notes between two parts to produce an effect of movement.

Ex. 5

A second way to avoid excessive repetition of a note is to use octave leaps, a device particularly useful in the Bass. Another solution to this problem is to combine several reiterated notes into a single tone of longer duration. Both of these devices are illustrated in the following examples, the Bass and Tenor parts respectively.

Ex. 6   "Winter Wonderland" — D. Smith and F. Bernard, arr. Arnaud - Naylor
© Copyright MCMXXXIV, Copyright renewed MCMXLVIII, Bregman, Vocco, & Conn, Inc.

Voice crossing

A device closely allied with these procedures is that of crossing the parts. This is usually done to maintain smooth, melodic voice leading, but has the further advantage of adding interest to the vocal lines of the harmony. In homophonic passages, Alto and Tenor may be crossed freely. However, crossing the Soprano and Alto is less desirable as there is danger of obscuring the melody. Similarly, crossing of Tenors below Basses confuses the bass line and is recommended only if Basses are not carrying the fundamental bass line of the harmonic structure. The example shows the common crossing of Alto and Tenor parts.

Ex. 7   "Requiem"—J. Brahms

In contrapuntal scoring there is complete freedom in crossing of voices. Here the parts are more nearly equal in melodic significance and there need be no concern about confusing the melodic line in the Soprano. Similarly, the Bass part is now primarily a melodic part and only secondarily furnishes the bass line of the harmonic structure.

(*Accompaniment duplicates vocal parts*)
Ex. 8   "The Seasons"—F. Haydn

Dividing the melody among various parts

Though this device is used mainly in writing for four-part male voices (T.T. B.B.) and will be discussed later in that section, it is occasionally useful in S.A. T.B. scoring. Discreetly employed, it adds interest to the writing, giving a more melodic character to inner parts. To avoid the danger of obscuring the melodic line, it is advisable to suggest, through a footnote, that a few "roving" voices be assigned to the melody throughout such an interchange.

Ex. 9   "Flow Gently Sweet Afton"

Chromatic and dissonant passages

The vocalist, unlike the player of a keyed instrument, must be able to hear mentally each pitch before sounding it. This circumstance imposes rather severe limitations upon the choral arranger in writing chromatic or dissonant passages. He must be acutely aware of vocalists' limitations in general, and particularly those of the group for whom he is writing. The tempo must be moderate enough to permit mental anticipation of all the intervals. In faster tempos there is little likelihood of satisfactory performance of chromatic and dissonant passages.

In chromatic passages which move rapidly, unison writing rather than harmonization is often the most effective as well as the most easily performed treatment.

Ex. 10

In writing dissonant passages, it is advisable to prepare the dissonant tones by including them in the previous chords. If such preparation is impracticable, approach the dissonance step-wise or by leaps no greater than a third.

Ex. 11

SUMMARY

The foregoing principles should serve as a guide in developing the ability to write choral parts that are singable and effective, and also achieve good choral balance. The experienced arranger will not be rigidly confined by these rules in all situations, but they should be carefully observed by the beginner. Gradually he will recognize with assurance those situations in which these principles may be safely disregarded.

The student must hear as many as possible of his own arrangements in performance, noting particularly any awkwardness of voice leading or muddiness of texture. Study of these passages will usually disclose a violation of one or more of the principles given here, and will indicate the necessary alterations. Adherence to this procedure for a reasonable length of time will result in a greatly improved command of the techniques of good part writing.

Reference or Study Suggestions

1. Review selections from standard repertoire as to how they illustrate part writing principles discussed in Chapter One.

2. Make a detailed analysis of a traditional (homophonic) composition showing the ways in which the following are effected:

   a) voice ranges
   b) use of close and open voicing
   c) doubling of notes within chords
   d) crossing of parts
   e) use of contrary motion

3. Study a contemporary arrangement by comparing the part writing with more traditional practices; itemize the differences and similarities.

CHAPTER 2

FOUR-PART WRITING

THE contemporary arranger will find that four-part writing, which through the centuries has been the principal medium for groups of voices, remains today his most valuable resource. However, several factors should be considered in deciding whether or not to use harmonization in four parts, rather than another type of choral treatment.

The first factor is tempo. The pace at which harmonic changes occur must be sufficiently moderate to insure that there is time for each chord to be clearly heard and understood. There must be time for the inner parts to register clearly or full harmonization becomes meaningless. In faster tempos, over-harmonization tends merely to muddy the texture and obscure the clarity of both melodic line and rhythmic movement.

Assuming a moderate tempo, four-part harmonization is the best medium for musical materials which are essentially dependent upon a complex harmonic structure. It should also be used with a simpler structure when the arranger wishes an effect of harmonic fullness and solidity rather than buoyancy and movement.

Though the principles discussed in this chapter apply in general to four-part writing for mixed, treble or male voices, their particular application here is to mixed voices. The special problems of writing for four-part male voices and four-part treble voices will be discussed in later chapters.

Unaccompanied four-part writing

Since the harmonic structure is fully represented, four-part writing may be either accompanied or unaccompanied, at the discretion of the arranger, whose choice will be dictated by the character of the music. In general, the materials best suited to unaccompanied treatment are those which do not require rhythmic support from an accompaniment to provide forward impetus.

The unmatched beauty and purity of the unaccompanied choral sound can be extremely effective for either entire works or as a contrasting section of an accompanied arrangement. (In the latter case, the unaccompanied section must be short enough to insure that the chorus will not experience intonation difficulties upon re-entrance of the accompaniment.)

Traditional four-part writing in serious music

Two settings of a classic hymn tune provide initial illustrations of four-part writing. The first is a straightforward homophonic setting such as is found in a contemporary hymnal. This treatment is, of course, particularly appropriate for congregational singing and is widely used in hymnals, community song books, and all other settings which require a sturdy and simple four-part sound. It is also the type of setting used in harmony texts.

Observe the freely continuing interchange between close and open voicing in this type of scoring. Observe also the presence of the Bass voices on the bass line of the harmonic structure. (See also Exs. 7, 9, 90, 105, 126, 209, 224, 282, 310.)

Ex. 12 "A Mighty Fortress Is Our God"—M. Luther

The second setting demonstates how, using the same material, the musical interest can be greatly increased with a more contrapuntal treatment by the great master of choral writing, J. S. Bach. The great effectiveness of such contrapuntal scoring arises from the melodic individuality of the vocal lines. (See also Ex. 153.)

Ex. 13   "Ein Feste Burg"—M. Luther, setting by J. S. Bach

The Bach chorales represent one of the high points of development in traditional four-part writing and universally are regarded as models of perfection in this style. The student will profit greatly from an extended study of these masterpieces.

The next few examples are drawn from other types of choral classics. In Ex. 14 note again the free alternation between open and close voicing whenever required by good voice leading; it also helps to avoid the monotony of tone color which might arise from continued use of either voicing. Furthermore, this alternation causes contrary motion at the points of interchange between voicings. With its balancing of upward and downward stresses, contrary motion produces the strong sense of structural stability which is an essential characteristic of this type of writing.

Observe the presence of the Bass voices on the bass line of the harmonic structure; this strengthens the feeling of harmonic solidity.

Ex. 14   "Requiem"—J. Brahms

Sometimes extended passages in either open or close voicing are used to achieve a particular effect. The choice of voicing in such cases should be determined by the nature of musical material and textural ideas. In Ex. 15, use of open voicing throughout produces the desired effect of breadth and sonority. Here the entire melody lies in a high register which demands open voicing for this passage to insure that the male voices do not rise above the register of their greatest depth and solidity.

Ex. 15   "Missa Solemnis"—L. van Beethoven

Ex. 16 illustrates the extended use of close voicing with a melodic line in a similarly high register. This voicing produces a more stentorian, declamatory quality because all voices are singing near the tops of their ranges. The intensity of the male vocal quality, in high register in particular, contributes to the dramatic effect of this scoring, which is most effective for strong, climactic passages and those suggesting a bright tone color.

Ex. 16   "Elijah" — F. Mendelssohn

Ex. 17 illustrates the extended use of close voicing in a passage with a register so low that alternation with open voicing is not practical. Such scoring is particularly effective for restful or sombre passages and those suggesting a dark tone color.

Ex. 17   "Requiem" — J. Brahms

Ex. 18 illustrates the extended use of an unusually close voicing in which the treble voice register is relatively low and that of male voices is high. This crowding together of the vocal parts results in a compact, closely knit grouping with strong resonance, even when performed quietly as in this example. The relative intensity of the male vocal quality in high register gives this voicing a highly effective sense of dramatic urgency.

Ex. 18   "A Sea Symphony" — R. Vaughan Williams
© Copyright MCMXVIII, Stainer and Bell, Ltd. Sole American Agent: Galaxy Music Corporation

Extended use of either open or close voicing may occasionally occur in medium register when the melodic line moves within a narrow range. This treatment is particularly applicable to quiet, unpretentious compositions in which the simple purity of the single voicing may heighten the charm of the passage, as in Ex. 19.

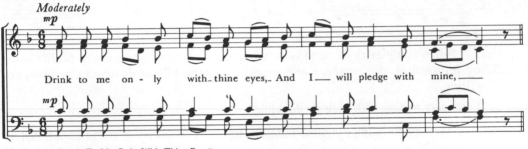

Ex. 19   "Drink To Me Only With Thine Eyes"

Traditional four-part writing in popular ballads and swing tunes

Traditional four-part writing can also serve as a satisfactory setting for popular songs. The passage from a popular ballad in Ex. 20 exhibits sufficient harmonic complexity and moves at a pace moderate enough to suggest full harmonization. Rich harmonization and judicious use of contrary motion combine to give this setting the warmth and richness demanded by the subject.

Ex. 20   "Over the Rainbow" — E.Y. Harburg, Harold Arlen
© Copyright MCMXXXIX, Leo Feist, Inc., New York, N.Y.,
Used by permission.

Traditional four-part harmonization is a useful form of simple voicing for swing tunes, because it permits easy, natural voice leading. Although the result is not a true "swing" sound, it is a satisfactory compromise for use with inexperienced groups.

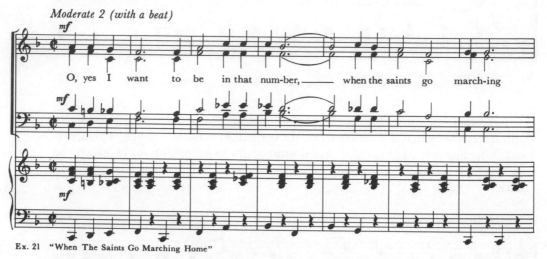

Ex. 21   "When The Saints Go Marching Home"

When complexity of melody or harmony makes continuous use of this voicing impractical, the arranger may resort to alternation with unison or two-part writing.

Four-part writing with melody doubling

Melody doubling by Alto, Tenor or Bass is a variation of traditional S.A.T.B. writing. It is most effective for music of relatively simple harmonic structure which does not require full four-part harmonization. In setting such materials, it may sometimes be advantageous to sacrifice full harmonization temporarily to strengthen the melody. Ex. 22 is a passage in which the Soprano melody is reinforced by Altos an octave lower.

Ex. 22   "Requiem" — G. Verdi

Ex .23 illustrates a similar treatment in which Tenors double the melodic line.

Ex. 23   "Alexander Nevsky" — S. Prokofieff

ⓒ Copyright MCMXLV, MCMXLIX, by LEEDS MUSIC CORPORATION
322 West 48th Street, New York 36, New York
Used by Permission   All Rights Reserved

Four-part writing in parallel motion

This is a style of vocal writing found increasingly in modern works. It is best adapted to vigorous, sweeping strains emphasizing movement, as in Ex. 24. Note that Bass voices double the melody. The omission from the vocal parts of the fundamental bass line of the harmonic structure gives an effect of lightness and buoyancy.

Ex. 24   "Cabeza de Vaca" — G. Antheil   ⓒ Copyright MCMLXI, Templeton Music Company, Inc.

Comparing this type of scoring with traditional harmonization is instructive. In the latter, its essential sense of structural strength results from two factors, (1) the judicious use of contrary motion, producing a balance between upward and downward stresses and imparting a strong feeling of structural stability, and (2) the presence of the Bass voices on the bass line of the harmonic structure, giving a sense of rock-bottom solidity. (See Exs. 3, 12, 14.)

When, however, the need is for buoyancy and movement, the opposite procedures are indicated. In such situations, omit the fundamental bass line from the vocal parts, assigning it to the accompaniment or dispensing with it entirely; instead of using the traditional contrary motion, let all the vocal parts move freely in parallel motion. Obviously, such writing in continuous parallel motion will preclude the alternation of close and open voicing, which is also basic traditional scoring. Nearly all four-part passages in parallel motion will be scored in continuous close voicing as this formation emphasizes buoyancy and movement better than open voicing. The foregoing principles are of basic importance to the effective setting of music of this type and they will be referred to frequently throughout this volume.

Ex. 25 is a setting of the same passage using traditional scoring, to illustrate its relative ineffectiveness for writing of this type. Observe that the repeated notes in the static bass part result in undesirable stiffness, and that the contrary motion seems to impede the smooth flow of forward movement.

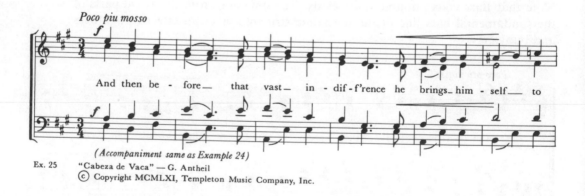

(*Accompaniment same as Example 24*)

Ex. 25   "Cabeza de Vaca" — G. Antheil
© Copyright MCMLXI, Templeton Music Company, Inc.

Ex. 26 illustrates the use of parallel motion by a contemporary French composer. Here again, traditional four-part writing is temporarily abandoned, and the melodic line doubled in the Bass voices. The fundamental bass is omitted almost entirely from both vocal parts and accompaniment.

Ex. 26   "Secheresses" — F. Poulenc
ⓒ Copyright MCMXXXIX, DURAND ET CIE, PARIS, copyright owners;
Elkan - Vogel Co., Philadelphia, Pa., agents.

Swing harmonization in parallel motion

This is the simplest form of true swing voicing and is particularly useful in writing for young or inexperienced groups for whom more complex voicings might prove difficult. The basic principle of this style of harmonization requires the use of four different tones in every chord without doubling any part, necessitating the addition of the major sixth to all triads, as on the first beat below. Passing tones are usually harmonized with diminished chords, as on the last half of the second beat. This procedure permits all parts to move, enhancing the unimpeded rhythmic sweep of the writing. Observe that in Ⓐ all parts move at each progression, while in Ⓑ the lower parts reiterate certain tones, detracting from the sense of vigorous rhythmic movement. Parallel motion is the basic pattern of scoring, but contrary motion may be introduced whenever suggested by the demands of smooth voice leading, as on the second beat of bar 4.

Ex. 26   "Mary -Had a Little Lamb"

Achieving color contrasts in S.A.T.B. writing

In some works for four-part mixed voices contrasting passages scored for other voicings provide effective variety. Such passages may be scored for any desired number of mixed, treble or male voices. Detailed discussion of these various voicings will be undertaken later in this book.

Ex. 27 illustrates such a contrasting passage in four-part writing for both male and treble voices. In the S.A.T.B. work from which the example is taken, this passage for male voices is repeated immediately by treble voices an octave higher, providing effective color contrast. The principles of scoring are generally the same as those for mixed voice writing, subject to certain range limitations.

Ex. 27 "Elijah" — F. Mendelssohn

SUMMARY

In this chapter we were primarily concerned with homophonic four-part writing, giving time to contrapuntal factors later in the book (Chapter Nine). Elements such as parallel motion, doubling, open and close voicing were presented as major points under arranging techniques. Four-part writing should be considered the basic medium for the choral arranger and from this foundation he can understand and develop innumerable combinations.

Reference or Study Suggestions

1. Using a chorale or hymn tune, write an unaccompanied traditional harmonization in four parts (S.A.T.B.).

2. Score a popular ballad using traditional part writing.

3. Score a popular rhythm tune, using parallel motion and swing harmonization.

4. Select for study several of the supplementary examples listed under Chapter 2 in the Appendix. Discuss the manner in which each composition reflects the principles of part writing as applied to four voices.

CHAPTER 3

ACCOMPANIMENTS

MANY choral settings cannot be satisfactorily arranged without the use of an accompaniment. Having presented the basic principles of part writing for voices, and applying these to four-part textures, discussion of accompaniment writing is now appropriate. This will provide the necessary background to study and practice scoring for all vocal combinations. Principles governing accompaniment writing will be explained through the use of piano and organ, the most commonly used instruments for accompanying. Scoring for other types of accompaniments will be found in Chapter Eighteen, "Chorus with Instrumental Groups."

The primary function of the accompaniment is to enhance the presentation of the musical and textual material of the arrangement. Fulfillment of this function may be achieved in any one or combination of the following ways: (1) reinforcing melodic line, (2) completing representation of the harmonic structure, (3) providing forward rhythmic impetus, (4) adding contrapuntal interest, (5) adding color through figuration or other forms of embellishment, (6) intensifying projection of the intellectual and emotional message of both text and music. Whichever means is chosen, the cardinal principle for accompaniments is that they must never overshadow the choral presentation. They always remain secondary, never assuming solo importance except in special instances where the arranger is setting a work or a passage as a piano solo with choral accompaniment. (See Ex. 52.)

METHODS

Styles of accompaniments

Obviously it would be impossible to catalog the infinite variety of accompaniment styles, but certain types do recur often enough to be classified: (1) accompaniments duplicating vocal parts, (2) rhythmic accompaniments, (3) melodic accompaniments, (4) sustained accompaniments, (5) punctuation as accompaniment, (6) arpeggiated accompaniments, (7) figuration as accompaniment, (8) contrapuntal accompaniments, (9) special effects in accompaniments, and (10) solo piano with choral accompaniment.

STYLES

Accompaniments duplicating vocal parts

The simplest accompaniments are those which merely duplicate or approximate the vocal parts. This treatment is particularly common with hymns, but may be utilized elsewhere when nothing more than reinforcement of the vocal parts is desired. Such duplication of voice parts is also scored in unaccompanied works in which voice parts appear on four or more staves. Such a voice condensation is usually shown in cue-size notes and marked "for rehearsal only."

Rhythmic accompaniments

There is a large group of accompaniment styles where the primary function is to maintain forward rhythmic impetus. In many cases, they also delineate the harmonic structure, but their basic purpose is rhythmic. These styles may vary greatly and are not limited to the patterns illustrated below. The arrranger should, however, be thoroughly familiar with these basic patterns from which may be developed variations suitable to the particular character of his musical materials. The melodic line is usually omitted from accompaniments whose primary function is rhythmic, as it tends to obscure both the rhythmic movement and clarity of melodic line in the vocal parts.

Ex. 28 Ⓐ shows the typical rhythmic chording pattern, commonly called "oom-pah" accompaniments. The after-beats in the right hand should be written in a medium register for solid rhythmic impact, the lowest notes no lower than F below middle C; and the highest no higher than B flat above middle C. The laws of smooth harmonic progression should be carefully observed and wide leaps avoided. Ex. 28 Ⓑ illustrates an unsuitable scoring of this style of accompaniment. (See Exs. 85, 135, 139, 150, 160, 162, 165, 218A, 246, 269.)

Ex. 28   "The Marines Hymn"

Ex. 29   "The Marines Hymn"

Ex. 29 illustrates another rhythmic accompaniment, this time with a strong bass counterpoint. Note that the after-beats are no longer necessary in the right hand because the rhythmic pattern is completely oulined in the bass figuration.

The following example illustrates the rhythmic chording for a swing tune in "cut" time. In faster tempos, this kind of accompaniment approximates the effect of Ex. 28. (See Exs. 21, 111, 148, 173, 237, 247.)

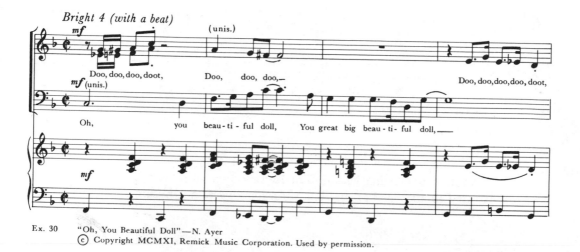

Ex. 30   "Oh, You Beautiful Doll"—N. Ayer
© Copyright MCMXI, Remick Music Corporation. Used by permission.

The rhythmic chording accompaniment may be varied by the adding of a counter melody in either hand, as below. (See Exs. 6, 140.)

Ex. 31   "An American Is a Very Lucky Man"—J. Roach
© Copyright MCMLVIII, Shawnee Press, Inc.

In left hand for most part on first beat of measure bass in Root position

Strong rhythmic movement may be achieved through the combination of after-beats in the right hand with a "walking" bass in the left. (See Exs. 26, 178.)

Ex. 32   "Loch Lomond" — arr. H. Ades

Another interesting variation of rhythmic chording is the "shuffle" rhythm illustrated in Ex. 33. For another variation of shuffle rhythm see Ex. 110.

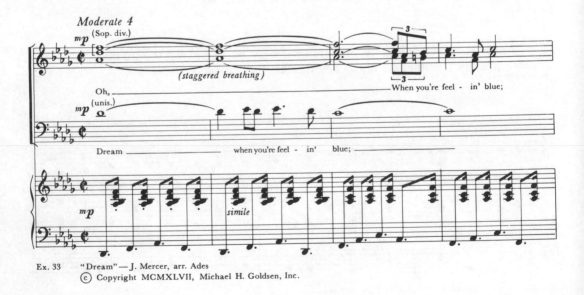

Ex. 33   "Dream" — J. Mercer, arr. Ades
          © Copyright MCMXLVII, Michael H. Goldsen, Inc.

A strong march rhythm may be achieved in 4/4 meter through the use of patterns such as the following.

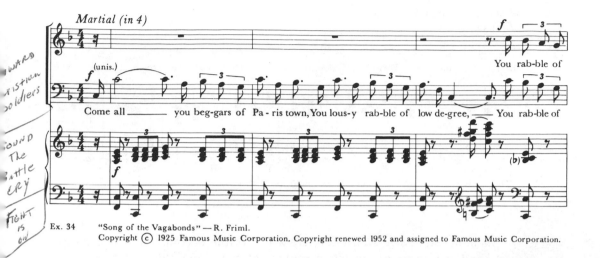

Ex. 34   "Song of the Vagabonds" — R. Friml.
Copyright ©C 1925 Famous Music Corporation. Copyright renewed 1952 and assigned to Famous Music Corporation.

The following formation, suggesting hoof beats, is particularly applicable to cowboy and Western songs.

Ex. 35   "Roll Along Covered Wagon" — J. Kennedy, arr. Ades
©C Copyright 1934 Peter Maurice Music Co. Ltd., London, England. Assigned 1935 for United States and Canada, to Irving Berlin, Inc., name changed to Bourne, Inc. Copyright renewed. This arrangement
©C Copyright 1959 Bourne, Inc. Used by Permission of Bourne Co.

Ex. 36 illustrates the basic waltz accompaniment style for lively tunes, in which the primary consideration is rhythmic impetus. The register and chord progression for the after-beats are the same as those for duple patterns.

Ex. 36   "The Sidewalks of New York" — Charles B. Lawlor and James W. Blake

In more expressive waltzes, where a less brittle accompaniment is desired, right hand chords are not merely repeated but move smoothly and more melodically.

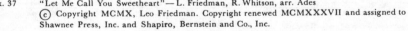

Ex. 37   "Let Me Call You Sweetheart" — L. Friedman, R. Whitson, arr. Ades
© Copyright MCMX, Leo Friedman. Copyright renewed MCMXXXVII and assigned to
Shawnee Press, Inc. and Shapiro, Bernstein and Co., Inc.

For a graceful rhythmic accompaniment for waltzes in moderate tempo, the chord on the third beat of each bar may be omitted. Note also the simple countermelody in the right hand.

Ex. 38   "Come Dance With Me" — D. Leibert, arr. Simeone
         © Copyright MCMLXI, MCMLI, Ben Bloom Music Corp.

Ex. 39 illustrates the typical Viennese waltz accompaniment style, characterized primarily by the anticipation of the second beat of each measure. (See Ex. 83.)

Ex. 39   "Wonderful Copenhagen" — F. Loesser, arr. Ades
         © Copyright 1951, 1952 by Frank Loesser. All Rights Reserved. Used by permission.

The normal pattern for marching rhythms in 6/8 meter is illustrated in Ex. 40.

An interesting variation of 6/8 rhythm is illustrated in Ex. 41. This treatment is extremely forceful and is particularly applicable to situations which call for strong rhythmic drive. (See Ex. 116.)

Ex. 40   "We're In the Navy" — F. Waring
          © Copyright MCMLVIII, Shawnee Press, Inc.

Ex. 41   "Nursery Rhyme Suite" — H. Simeone
          © Copyright MCMXLVII, Shawnee Press, Inc.

For powerful maestoso passages an accompaniment using triplets in 4/4 meter is highly effective as in Ex. 42. Such accompaniments are frequently scored in 12/8. (See Exs. 218 C, 253.)

Ex. 42 is but one variant of a group of accompaniments less obviously rhythmic than those previously discussed but whose primary function is still to supply rhythmic impetus. These accompaniments are based on repeated chord formations in simple rhythmic patterns, and may vary in dynamic range from the gentlest pianissimo to the strongest fortissimo, depending on the musical and textual idea. Ex. 43 illustrates a dynamic level opposite to that of Ex. 42. (See Exs. 75, 79, 91, 128, 133.)

Ex. 42   "The Almighty" — F. Schubert

Ex. 43   "The Creation" — F. Haydn

Latin-American music provides numerous rhythmic patterns for which there are many possible variations. The following examples illustrate the basic patterns for the better known Latin-American rhythms. The student should study the characteristics of this style and exercise his ingenuity in devising variations suitable to the music with which he is working.

BEGUINE
Moderate 4

Melodic accompaniments

When rhythmic emphasis is not a primary concern, a fairly complete representation of the musical material is often used. This may include the melodic line as well as the basic harmonic and rhythmic elements. The melodic line in the accompaniment often is an approximation rather than an exact restatement of the melody. In Ex. 44, the alterations in the first measure take advantage of pianistic style, and the figurations in measures 2 and 4 are added where the melody is static. Observe also that in measures 1 and 2 the melodic line in both accompaniment and choral parts are in the same register, whereas in measures 3 and 4 the accompaniment rises to the upper octave. Extended melodic accompaniments may be written in either register. (See Exs. 14, 24, 27, 53, 71, 80, 131 B, 175, 181, 201, 206, 208.)

Ex. 44 "The Seasons" — F. Haydn

Sustained accompaniments

This type of accompaniment is often employed to supply the harmonic structure, particularly with free-moving melodies. These accompaniments usually exhibit a degree of movement to complement that of the melodic line. A sustained melody is best suited by a moving accompaniment, while a florid melody suggests a sustained accompaniment as in Ex. 45. (See Exs. 55, 69, 104, 182, 202, 230, 241, 249.)

Ex. 45 "Cape Cod Chantey" —arr. L. Gearhart

Duplication of choral accompaniment for a solo voice or section is another use of the sustained accompaniment.

Ex. 46 "This Is My Father's World"—B. Maltby, arr. Ringwald

Punctuation as accompaniment

Short chords may be used to punctuate and outline the harmonic and rhythmic structure of the music, particularly if the melody is fast moving. This accompaniment has the added virtue of enhancing the clarity of the song text. (See Exs. 77-A, 172, 254.)

Ex. 47 "The Song of America" — R. Ringwald
© Copyright MCMLI, Shawnee Press, Inc.

Arpeggiated accompaniments

Using the harmonic structure as broken chords or arpeggios is the basis for another style of accompaniment. This treatment is particularly good with flowing melodies, and our example illustrates how this technique is used effectively. This type of accompaniment frequently serves as an introduction, as in the example. (See Exs. 15, 118, 255.)

Ex. 48 "O Holy Night" — A. Adam

Figuration as accompaniment

In this accompaniment style, a figure is repeated exactly or closely imitated. In Ex. 49 the flowing eighth-note figuration is appropriate to the character of the music and the text. As in arpeggiated accompaniments, figurations may be used as introductory material. In this instance, three bars of figuration precede the choral entrance. (See Exs. 90, 95, 134, 174, 194, 203, 222, 272.)

Ex. 49 "Mass in B-minor" — J. S. Bach

Contrapuntal accompaniments

Contrapuntal accompaniments use countermelodies so strongly delineated that the arrangement becomes polyphonic rather than homophonic. Here considerable discretion is needed to insure that the countermelody does not obscure or overshadow the main material of the arrangement. The accompaniment in Ex. 50 illustrates the approximate limit of importance which can safely be assumed by a countermelody. (See Exs. 22, 23, 62, 74, 93, 170.)

Ex. 50 "Requiem" — J. Brahms

Special effects in accompaniment

Other special accompanying effects are so numerous as to defy any attempt at classification. Most of these are derived from an object or idea expressed or implied in the text. Many of them are directly imitative of natural sounds, as in Ex. 51, which obviously imitates the sound of chimes. (See Exs. 54, 57, 82⁻A, 117, 119, 123, 137, 138, 231⁻B, 270.)

Ex. 51 "Ring Those Christmas Bells" — G. Levene, arr. H. Ades
ⓒ Copyright MCMLII, Shawnee Press, Inc.

Solo piano with choral accompaniment

Effective contrast is occasionally afforded by setting a portion of an arrangement for solo piano with choral accompaniment, using neutral vocal sounds for the choral accompaniment, to insure its subordination to the solo piano part, as in Ex. 52.

An important consideration for all styles of accompaniment is the treatment of the bass line. As discussed earlier it is often desirable, if movement and buoyancy are to be the main characteristics of the setting, to have the Bass voices sing a part other than the fundamental bass line, and assign this to the accompaniment. In such cases the Bass voice part and the bass line of the accompaniment will not coincide. However, when Bass voices are singing the bass line of the harmonic structure, this should coincide with the bass line of the accompaniment in order to avoid confusion as to which constitutes the true bass. Ex. 53 shows correct and incorrect accompaniment bass lines.

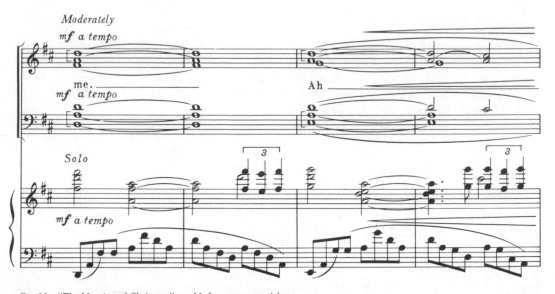

Ex. 52 "The Meaning of Christmas" — M. Lawrence, arr. Ades
© Copyright MCMLXI, Empress Music, Inc. All Rights Reserved.
Used by permission.

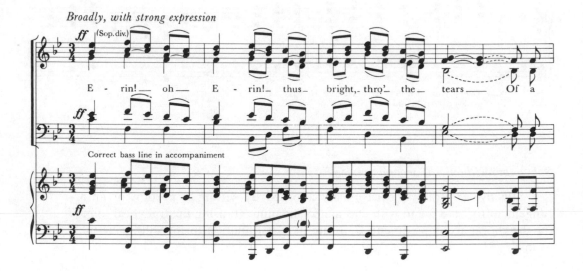

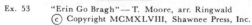

Ex. 53 "Erin Go Bragh" — T. Moore, arr. Ringwald
© Copyright MCMXLVIII, Shawnee Press, Inc.

This principle does not apply, of course, when the register of the accompaniment is high enough to preclude the possibility of confusion with the bass line in the vocal parts.

Ex. 54   "Jingle Bells"

All the accompaniment styles we have considered may, of course, be used freely for interest and variety. How long any particular style or combination of styles should be used will be determined by the character of the music; the accompaniment styles must always be appropriate to the music's expressive intent.

Four-hand accompaniments for one piano

Four-hand accompaniments provide a greatly increased range of color and dynamic resources which makes them particularly useful in more complex, ambitious arrangements. Although the basic principles for two-hand accompaniments also apply to four-hand accompaniments, the arranger should not undertake scoring for four hands until he has acquired assurance in handling the simpler form. (See Exs. 106, 142, 235.)

Two-piano accompaniments

Scoring accompaniments for two pianos offers the opportunity to approximate still more closely the full resources of the orchestra. Unfortunately, however, few choral groups have two pianos available. Scoring for two pianos should be attempted only by those with considerable experience in writing for the instrument.

Organ as accompaniment

Scoring accompaniments for organ generally follows the same principles that apply to the piano. All the categories of accompaniment style discussed previously are available, although with varying degrees of effectiveness.

Rhythmic — *NOT GOOD on Organ*

Accompaniments of the brittle, percussive variety, illustrated in Exs. 28, 30, are relatively ineffective on the pipe organ and should be avoided. Fortunately, little music requiring such accompaniments is likely to be performed where only a pipe organ is available. This limitation on rhythmic accompaniments does not apply to the electronic organ, which is a more percussive instrument.

Sustained — *GOOD use of ORGAN*

These are particularly effective on the organ, since the most important distinction between that instrument and the piano is its ability to sustain. The arranger should be aware of this possibility, and should exploit it to the fullest extent, as in Ex. 55.

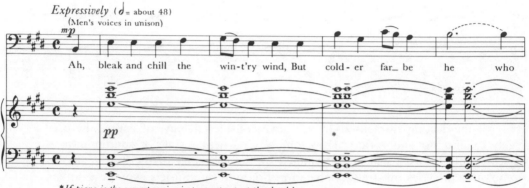

*If piano is the accompanying instrument, repeat the chord here

Ex. 55   "Ah, Bleak and Chill the Wintry Wind" — words by Bates G. Burt, music by Alfred Burt, arr. Ades
© Copyright MCMLIV, MCMLVIII, Hollis Music, Inc., New York, New York

Arpeggiated

Since the organ lacks the sustaining pedal of the piano, arpeggiated accompaniments are apt to sound thin and sketchy unless written to indicate the sustaining of each note in each chord. For instance, the arpeggiated accompaniment of Ex. 48 should be scored for organ as shown in Ex. 56.

Ex. 56   "O Holy Night" — A. Adam

NO Wide leaps

Another problem which arises from the absence of sustaining pedal on the organ is that wide leaps which require lifting all the fingers from the keyboard cannot be connected and therefore sound awkward and disjointed. Ex. 57 shows such a piano accompaniment and its adaptation for organ.

Ex. 57   "Christ Was Born on Christmas Day"

Scoring techniques

In scoring accompaniments for organ, two staves are usually adequate. The addition of a third staff for pedals is required only in elaborate accompaniments and should be attempted only by those thoroughly acquainted with the techniques of organ scoring.

Unless otherwise indicated, it is assumed in all two-stave organ parts that the pedals will play the bottom notes of the staff. Where it is desired that a passage be played without pedals, "Manuals only" is placed at the beginning of the passage with the word "Pedal" at the re-entrance of the pedals.

When it is necessary to indicate specific notes to be played on pedals, use up-stems for manuals and down-stems for pedals, as shown in Ex.58.

Ex. 58   "Oh, Who Are These That Throng the Way" (All on a Christmas Morning), words by Bates G. Burt,
music by Alfred Burt, arr. Ades. © Copyright MCMLIV, MCMLVIII, Hollis Music, Inc., New York, New York

Unless the arranger is an experienced organist, it is usually wiser not to attempt specific directions for registration. The dynamic markings and general character of the music will be adequate guides to the organist in choosing a registration suitable to his particular instrument.

SUMMARY

The extensive classification of accompaniments in Chapter Three is an indication of the important place it holds in writing for choral groups. Any one facet of accompanying techniques, Latin-American figures for example, may provide the major rhythmic interest for an entire arrangement. Use of the organ requires special preparation and knowledge, as do more complex four-hand and two-piano accompaniments.

Reference and Study Suggestions

1. Making use of the list of supplementary examples in the Appendix, find several compositions which illustrate various styles of accompaniments. Show how well each accomplishes a specific purpose.

2. Write suitable piano accompaniments for folk tunes which call for characteristic types, such as: *Down in the valley, Turkey in the Straw, Blow the Man Down, Loch Lomond, The Erie Canal.*

3. Select a Western cowboy tune, a Latin-American song, or some other definite type, as the basis for an S.A.T.B. arrangement with piano accompaniment.

CHAPTER 4

THREE-PART WRITING

THREE-PART writing is used in two main areas: (1) to score contrasting passages in S.A.T.B. writing and (2) in writing for choruses with only three voice sections — treble choruses (S.S.A.), mixed choruses with only one male voice part (S.A.B.) and male voice choruses (T.B.B., or more rarely T.T.B.). Although the principles are largely the same, whichever purpose is served, this chapter will discuss specifically the writing of contrasting passages within S.A.T.B. arrangements. The specific problems relating to three-part choruses are discussed in detail in chapters on treble and male voice choruses. (See Chapters Eleven and Twelve.)

Traditional three-part writing

Traditional three-part writing, like four-part writing, utilizes the principles of contrary motion and free interchange between open and close voicing. (In close voicing, the three vocal parts lie within an octave, while in open voicing they span an interval greater than an octave.) The bass line of the harmonic structure may or may not be included in the voice parts, depending upon circumstances discussed in this chapter.

Unaccompanied traditional three-part writing

Since three-part writing does not provide complete representation of the harmonic structure, writing extended unaccompanied passages requires particular effort to achieve the effect of complete harmonization. This is best accomplished by using an approximation of the fundamental bass as the lowest voice part.

Ex. 59 illustrates the scoring of an unaccompanied passage for the upper three voices in an S.A.T.B. work. Such passages in mixed voice scoring give a charming effect of purity and simplicity, which contrasts effectively with the fully harmonized sections.

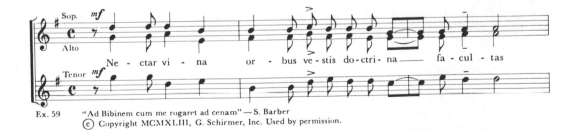

Ex. 59 "Ad Bibinem cum me rogaret ad cenam" — S. Barber
© Copyright MCMXLIII, G. Schirmer, Inc. Used by permission.

Ex. 60, illustrating unaccompanied three-part writing for treble voices alone, uses a combination of open and close voicing. In this instance, the composer set a complete section for unaccompanied treble voices within an oratorio for mixed voices. The writing is a model of perfection and the student will profit greatly from careful study of it. Observe that in the absence of accompaniment, care is taken to include in the lower vocal part an approximation of the bass line of the harmonic structure, even though only treble voices are used. The result closely approaches the effect of complete harmonization.

Ex. 60   "Elijah" — F. Mendelssohn

Ex. 61, from a contemporary work, illustrates scoring for unaccompanied male voices in three parts. Note the stark harmonization on the third beats of bars 1 and 2, and the free use of consecutive fifths in the lower parts. Though these devices are typical of modern writing, the basic principles of traditional three-part writing are plainly evident in the emphasis upon contrary motion, alternation of open and close voicing, and inclusion of the fundamental bass.

Ex. 61   "Songs of Conquest" — H. McDonald
ⓒ Copyright MCMXXXVII, MCMXXXIX, Elkan - Vogel Co., Inc.
Elkan - Vogel Company, Co., copyright owners, Philadelphia, Pa.

Accompanied traditional three-part writing

There are two basic types of traditional three-part scoring in accompanied passages: (1) scoring using the fundamental bass line in the vocal parts, and (2) scoring with this line used in the accompaniment or omitted entirely. In the first, and more usual type, the general principles are the same as for unaccompanied writing, with alternation of open and close voicing, and inclusion of the true bass line in the lowest vocal part.

Where only three of the four sections of the mixed chorus are used, usually adjacent parts, S.A.T. or A.T.B., are chosen. In Ex. 62, the Bass voices were omitted with a resulting brightening of tone color for this contrasting passage.

Ex. 62   "Messiah" — G. Handel

Ex. 63 illustrates the second type of traditional three-part scoring for accompanied mixed voices, where range limitations and the general outline of the harmony make impractical the inclusion of the bass line in the lower vocal part. Observe, however, that contrary motion and alternation of close and open voicing are retained. In such passages, the voices should be regarded as comprising the upper three parts of a harmonic structure, with the fourth part either expressed or implied in the accompaniment.

Ex. 63   "Barba Garibo" — D. Milhaud
(c) Copyright MCMLV, Heugel & Cie

Alternation of close and open voicing is also usual in writing for accompanied three-part treble voices. The fundamental bass line may or may not be included in the Bass part, depending upon range considerations and the character of the composition. In Ex. 64 the bass line is included for maximum solidity and sonority.

Ex. 64   "Messiah" — G. Handel

Ex. 65 illustrates an accompanied passage for three-part treble voices in which it was inadvisable to include the bass line of the harmony (pedal point C) in the vocal parts. To do so would have resulted in undesirable thinness of the vocal sonorities. Note that the traditional use of contrary motion is retained.

Ex. 65   "La Prima Vera" — O. Respighi
ⓒ Copyright MCMXXIII. Universal - Edition

The same general principles apply to traditional scoring of accompanied passages for three-part male voices.

Three-part writing in parallel motion

As with four-part scoring, parallel motion is most useful in setting ideas suggesting emphasis on buoyancy and movement. In such material, solidity of structure is of secondary importance, and the sweeping movement of the melodic line is reinforced by allowing the accompanying voices to proceed in the same direction. This type of scoring was used only sparingly by earlier composers, and is a relatively recent development in choral writing.

Either close or open voicing may be used in such passages for mixed voices but interchanges between the two are infrequent, as the opportunity is greatly limited by the very nature of parallel motion.

Ex. 66 illustrates the use of open voicing in an unaccompanied three-part passage for mixed voices·in parallel motion. The dramatic effect of the bold leaps in the melodic line is enhanced by parallel leaps in the accompanying parts.

Ex. 66   "Love Song"—anon.

Ex. 67 illustrates a more conventional use of open voicing in an accompanied three-part passage for mixed voices in parallel motion. In this passage inclusion of the bass line of the harmony in the vocal parts would overly thicken the choral texture and detract from the sense of movement. For that reason, it is assigned to the accompaniment.

Ex. 67   "Barba Garibo"—D. Milhaud
          © Copyright MCMLV, Heugel & Cie

Ex. 68 illustrates a three-part passage for mixed voices in close voicing in parallel motion. Note here the use of uninterrupted parallel motion in a passage which closely approaches the effect of an unaccompanied passage. Observe also the free use of consecutive fifths.

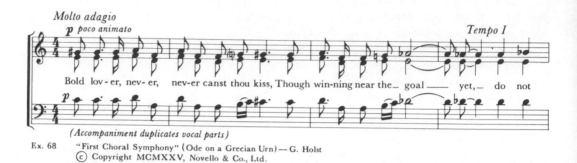

(*Accompaniment duplicates vocal parts*)

Ex. 68   "First Choral Symphony" (Ode on a Grecian Urn) — G. Holst
© Copyright MCMXXV, Novello & Co., Ltd.

Ex. 69 presents another form of three-part writing for mixed voices in parallel motion — male voices doubling Sopranos in the lower octave. This device is useful to strengthen the melodic line.

Ex. 69   "Hear the Heavenly Child Is Born" — arr. H. Ades
© Copyright MCMLIX, Shawnee Press, Inc.

Ex. 70 illustrates close voicing in an unaccompanied passage for treble voices in parallel motion. Because of range limitations, close voicing is almost invariably used in such passages for male or treble voices alone. Parallel motion effectively enhances the fanfare-like quality of this contrasting passage from a work for mixed voices.

Ex. 70   "A Sea Symphony" — R. Vaughan Williams
© Copyright MCMXVIII, Stainer and Bell, Ltd. Sole American Agent: Galaxy Music Corp.

Ex. 71 illustrates close voicing in an accompanied passage for three-part treble voices in parallel motion. Since movement is desired, the bass line of the harmonic structure is not included in the vocal parts but is approximated in the accompaniment.

This example, taken from a work for mixed voices, was scored for treble voices alone in keeping with the text.

Ex. 71   "First Choral Symphony" -- G. Holst
© Copyright MCMXXV, Novello & Co., Ltd.

Ex. 72 illustrates close voicing in three-part parallel motion for male voices in an unaccompanied passage, in which the robust quality of male voices is particularly appropriate. Choice of this combination of voices at this point in an arrangement for mixed voices was obviously dictated by the character of the musical and lyric ideas to be projected.

Ex. 72   "The Unicorn, the Gorgon and the Manticore"—G. Menotti
ⓒ Copyright MCMLVI, MCMVII, G. Ricordi & Co., New York
By permission of Franco Colombo, Inc., New York

SUMMARY

Traditional three-part writing, as with four-part, stresses contrary motion and a continuing interchange between close and open voicing. Care must be taken in unaccompanied three-part passages to represent as closely as possible the complete harmonic structure, usually including tne bass line of the harmony in the vocal parts. In accompanied passages in traditional style, however, the bass line may or may not be included in the vocal parts, depending upon range limitations and the character of the music. Three-part writing in parallel motion offers a wide range of opportunities for effective setting of contrasting passages emphasizing buoyancy and movement. Three-part writing is a valuable color resource in S.A.T.B. scoring.

Reference and Study Suggestions

1. Score a traditional melody with text, a chorale or an old carol, for three equal voices; set a stylized accompaniment (See Chapter Three) to the arrangement.

2. For male voices without accompaniment, write a three part version of Praetorius' *Lo, How a Rose E'er Blooming*. The harmonic structure should be as simple as is customarily used for this music.

3. Write a short passage for unaccompanied treble voices which illustrates close voicing in parallel motion. Use a neutral syllable and devise your own melodic ideas.

CHAPTER 5

TWO-PART WRITING

TWO-PART writing, like three-part writing, serves two main purposes: (1) as the medium for choruses in which only two parts are available — treble choruses (S.A.), mixed choruses (S.B.), and male choruses (T.B.) and (2) for contrasting passages within S.A.T.B. writing. The basic principles are the same whichever medium is served. These principles are discussed in relation to contrasting passages within S.A.T.B. scoring. Two-part writing for treble, male voices and mixed voices is discussed in detail in later chapters. (See Chapters Ten, Eleven and Twelve.)

Traditional two-part writing

Traditional two-part writing is less clearly defined than either three- or four-part writing. One reason is that the smaller number of parts reduces opportunity to include the bass line of the harmonic structure within the vocal parts. Nevertheless, the basic outlines of traditional style are clearly evident in the works of classical composers. Contrary motion is used wherever practical, and there is frequently included in the lowest vocal part an approximation of the bass line of the harmony.

Unaccompanied traditional two-part writing

Since two-part writing is dependent to a considerable degree upon the accompaniment for the harmonies, unaccompanied passages should be comparatively short, unless an unusual effect is desired. As with four- and three-part writing, traditional two-part scoring is particularly valuable in unaccompanied passages. It provides a feeling of balance and solidity giving the effect of a more complete harmonic structure, and thereby diminishes dependence upon the accompaniment.

Traditional two-part writing usually employs only unisons, thirds, fifths, sixths, octaves and tenths. (Seconds fourths and sevenths are used freely in contemporary writing.) Occasional intervals greater than an octave are not objectionable in traditional two-part writing, as the very nature of contrary motion precludes continuance of wide intervals between the parts.

Ex. 73 illustrates the application of these principles in an unaccompanied passage for mixed voices.

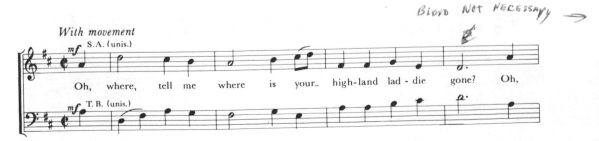

Ex. 73   "The Blue Bells of Scotland"

Accompanied traditional two-part writing

Passages in traditional style are frequently scored for two-part groupings of mixed voices, usually S.T., A.T., or A.B. Ex. 74 illustrates an accompanied passage of this type for Soprano and Tenor voices. The wide spacing in measures 2 and 4 is temporary, therefore not objectionable. In such circumstances, use of alternately wide and close spacing adds interest.

In accompanied two-part passages in traditional style, whether the bass line is included in the vocal parts depends upon the character of the music and the effect desired. In Ex. 74 the bass line is omitted to achieve lightness and grace.

Ex. 74   "The Seasons" — F. Haydn

Ex. 75   "Alexander Nevsky" — S. Prokofieff

© Copyright MCMXLV, MCMXLIX, by LEEDS MUSIC CORPORATION
322 West 48th Street, New York 36, New York
Used by Permission   All Rights Reserved

Ex. 75 illustrates traditional two-part writing for treble voices alone. Observe the interesting alternation of two-part with three-part writing at points where the melodic line is relatively sustained. Such alternation of voicings can be highly effective.

Ex. 76 illustrates scoring a passage for male voices alone as color contrast in a work for mixed voices. Use of contrary motion permits inclusion of the fundamental bass which provides great solidity and sonority.

Ex. 76 "The Messiah" —G. Handel

Traditional two-part writing in octaves

Passages scored for two-part treble voices with male voices in two-parts an octave below may be regarded as an extension of two-part writing, even though there are four vocal lines. (See Exs. 39, 82-A, 141, 157-A.)

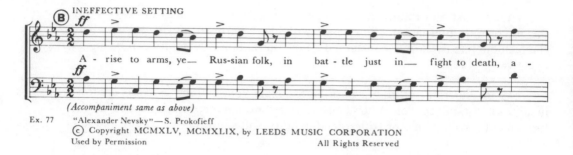

Ex. 77 "Alexander Nevsky"—S. Prokofieff
ⓒ Copyright MCMXLV, MCMXLIX, by LEEDS MUSIC CORPORATION
Used by Permission   All Rights Reserved

The vigorous theme in Ex. 77A, as set for duplicated two-part voices, is far more effective than it would have been if scored for male or treble voices alone or if all treble voices had been assigned to the melody and all male voices to the harmony as in 77B. In the latter case, the wide spacing produces a hollow effect unsuitable to the strong character of the theme.

Parallel two-part writing

Materials best suited to two-part writing in parallel motion are those which require lightness and motion rather than solidity of structure. The most normal harmonizations for such passages are thirds, sixths, or "horncall" patterns although other intervals are used increasingly in modern scoring.

Ex. 78 illustrates two-part scoring for mixed voices in a passage, suitably harmonized in sixths throughout. The bass line of the fundamental harmony is omitted as its inclusion would result in an unpleasantly thin harmonization. Adequate representation of the bass line is provided by the accompaniment.

Ex. 78   "Poor Little Baby Jesus"—arr. H. Ades

In settings of this type the peculiarity of male voice timbre (See page 4, Chapter 1.) will often give the impression that the male voices are singing the harmony part a third higher, rather than a sixth below the melody. This illusion actually enhances the effect of such passages, particularly if they are nostalgic or sentimental in character.

Similar themes may be scored for treble or male voices alone when the melody lies in a comfortable register. For instance, the vocal parts of Ex. 78 could be effectively scored for treble voices a fourth higher or male voices a fourth lower.

Ex. 79 illustrates a similar passage for Altos and Tenors, Mixed voice formations of this type can be effectively scored S.T., A.T., or A.B. (See Ex. 74.) This passage represents the first voice entrance in a major work for chorus and orchestra, showing the composer's concern for color variety.

Ex. 79   "Alexander Nevsky" — S. Prokofieff

ⓒ Copyright MCMXLV, MCMXLIX, by LEEDS MUSIC CORPORATION
322 West 48th Street, New York 36, New York
Used by Permission   All Rights Reserved

Ex. 80   "From the Bavarian Highlands" — E. Elgar

As in other voicings, parallel motion is particularly effective in treating materials that are active and buoyant, as illustrated in Ex. 80, scored for treble voices alone. Harmonization in thirds using parallel motion is common in two-part writing.

The first four bars of Ex. 81 are scored in parallel motion in thirds for male voices alone. Observe in bars 5-7 the interesting formation in which male voices continue in thirds, while treble voices in thirds are added in contrary motion. Alternation of two-part writing with other forms is a basic means of achieving color variety in S.A.T.B. scoring.

Ex. 81   "Missa Solemnis" -- L. van Beethoven

Parallel motion in octaves

As with Ex. 77, the four vocal lines in Ex. 82A represent two-part writing in octaves. (See Exs. 141, 157A, 235-Letter G.)

(*Piano accompaniment same as above*)

Ex. 82   "The Stars and Stripes" — J. Sousa

The same material, set as in Ex. 82B would be less satisfactory, because the maintenance of an interval greater than an octave between the parts results in a bare and empty effect not suitable to this stirring march.

Ex. 83 illustrates the use of octaves in material suitably harmonized in sixths. In such settings, the melody must lie in relatively high range, to avoid forcing the harmony parts too low, resulting in an unpleasantly "growly" texture.

Ex. 83   "Tales of the Vienna Woods" — J. Strauss

Ex. 84 illustrates the two-part "horn-call" harmonization in octaves. Observe the change from two-part writing in measures 1-2 to traditional four-part harmonization in measures 3-4. Such alternation of simple voicings with fully harmonized sections can prove highly effective.

Ex. 84   "Onward Christian Soldiers" — A. Sullivan, arr. H. Simeone
© Copyright MCMXLIII, Shawnee Press, Inc.

SUMMARY

Two-part writing is used for two-part choruses and to achieve color variety in S.A.T.B. scoring. Through examples and suggestions, we have explored ·adi- tional scoring for mixed, treble, and male voices. Attention was given to the use of parallel motion in two parts and the way in which extensions involve oc- tave duplications. Two-part writing is a simple means of gaining interest and variety; it is also completely satisfying as a basic vocal combination.

Reference and Study Suggestions

1. Arrange the French Carol *Angels We Have Heard on High* for two parts (S.B.) with an appropriate accompaniment.

2. Score *Vive L'amour*, or a similar song, for two-part male voices using one of the rhythmic style accompaniments discussed in Chapter Three.

3. Find several compositions or arrangements where a two-part texture is used even when writing for multiple voices. Refer to the supplementary ex- amples at the back of the book.

CHAPTER 6

UNISON WRITING

THE unison is one of the most valuable resources available to the arranger, and one of the most neglected. This neglect probably arises because the inexperienced arranger becomes completely engrossed with the myriad fascinating possibilities in harmonic combinations.

Use of the unison is one of the most practical ways of achieving variety in choral writing. The full chorus unison is the strongest single sound available to the arranger, with the possible exception of a chord so placed that each of the four voices sounds in its most powerful register. This fact is well recognized among radio, television, and recording engineers who are confronted with the problem of securing a balance of sound between chorus and orchestral accompaniment.

In addition, the unison is extremely flexible and adapts itself to almost any type of music. The few exceptions where unison writing is not appropriate will be noted later. Best of all, particularly from the viewpoint of those working with young or inexperienced groups, unison writing is easily learned and performed. It is a happy coincidence that one of the most effective resources in choral writing is also the easiest to perform.

Melodies which best lend themselves to unison treatment are those with simple harmonies and which do not depend primarily upon a complex harmonic background for their essential character. Where the harmonic structure is simple, it need not be spelled out completely in the vocal parts; it will be implied by the melody itself if unaccompanied, or may be assigned to the accompaniment.

Strong melodic line

Our first unison example is a strong, sharply outlined melody. The unison provides a bold and powerful means of stating such a theme, the cleanness of the unison line permitting the rhythmic accompaniment to register clearly and provide the sense of movement needed by the sustained melody.

Ex. 85   "This Is My Country" — A. Jacobs
© Copyright MCMXL, MCMXLVI, Shawnee Press, Inc.

Ex. 86A illustrates another strong melodic line well adapted to unison treatment. Scoring of this sort is effective in melodic lines which spell out chords, as in measure 1-2, 5-6. Observe in 86B how much less forceful harmonization of this same passage would have been. Even the employment of contrary motion in Bars 1-2, 5-6 does not match the strength and vigor of the pure unison. Furthermore, the unison setting permits greater color variety, through alternation with harmonized sections. This technique will be considered later in greater detail.

Ex. 86   "The Heavens Resound"— L. van Beethoven

Comparison of Exs. 87A and B will underline the importance of recognizing that some melodies suggest unison treatment and others do not. Whereas harmonization detracts from the forcefulness of measure 1-3, it is almost vital in measure 4, where the sub-dominant to tonic relationship gives added stress at beats 1-3.

Ex. 87   "Messiah" — G. Handel

Flowing melodic line

The second type of melodic unison is broad and flowing, in contrast to the sharper outline of the first. Such melodic lines are warm and expressive, but still simple enough in harmonic structure to be practical in unison. Ex. 88 illustrates particularly well that unison in both vocal parts and accompaniment may be effective. In this instance, the accompaniment is merely a duplication of the choral unison, with a result approximating the effect of an unaccompanied setting. Despite the complete absence of harmonization, this pattern of writing is convincingly continued for thirteen measures beyond the passage illustrated in Ex. 88.

This example also illustrates one of the numerous variations of the unison pattern, several more of which will be discussed under subsequent examples. Note that the women's voices are written in unison, while the Tenors are written in the upper octave rather than in strict unison with the Basses. This procedure will usually prove expedient in avoiding range problems where the melody is relatively low. Also, the brightness of the Tenor part in the upper octave helps to avoid an unduly dark tone color.

Ex. 88   "Requiem" — G. Verdi

Rhythmic melodic line

This is a melodic line of still different character, vigorously moving and rhythmic in itself. In Ex. 89, a typical swing tune, the rhythmic accompaniment must register cleanly to provide forward impetus. (See Ex. 98.) Harmonization here, besides adding performance difficulty, detracts from the strength and vigor of this melody.

Ex. 89B is a traditional harmonization of the same melody. Since chord changes are relatively infrequent, the inner voices tend to reiterate the same notes, producing an undesired static effect where a sense of movement is wanted.

Even a typical swing harmonization, as in 89C, is weaker than the unison treatment. The rapid movement of vocal parts obscures the registering of harmonic progressions. Furthermore, the singer's difficulty with the harmony parts will tend to produce a somewhat cumbersome effect. Here harmonization merely muddies the texture and impedes rhythmic drive.

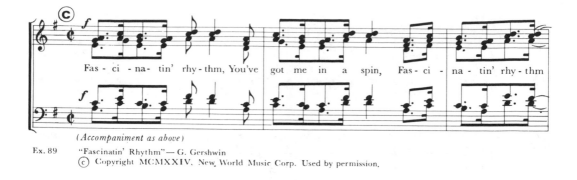

(*Accompaniment as above*)

Ex. 89   "Fascinatin' Rhythm" — G. Gershwin
      © Copyright MCMXXIV, New World Music Corp. Used by permission.

The rhythmic unison is applicable to a wide range of music. Ex. 90 represents still another of its numerous variations. Here the passage was set for Sopranos and Tenors only, because of the relatively high range of the passage. In other situations, unisons might well be written for Altos and Basses alone, for either women's or men's voices alone, or for any single group of voices. The choice in such matters will depend upon the range and character of the musical material. (See Exs. 91, 94.)

Ex. 90   "First Choral Symphony" — G. Holst
      © Copyright MCMXXV, Novello & Co., Ltd.

Unison as recitative

Unison is by far the most commonly used choral setting for parlando passages, since it most closely parallels the effect of a solo voice. Opportunities for use of this technique are found mainly in serious or sacred music as in Ex. 91, scored for Altos and Tenors alone. This relatively unusual grouping of voices represents still another variation of unison writing.

Ex. 91   "Symphonie des Psaumes" — I. Stravinsky
Copyright 1931 by Russischer Musikverlag; Renewed 1958. Copyright and renewal
assigned to Boosey & Hawkes Inc. Revised version copyright 1948 by Boosey & Hawkes, Inc. Reprint by permission.

Unison melodic lines in high range

When the melodic line rises beyond a comfortable range for Altos and Basses, octaves are used in each staff, resulting in a three-octave pattern. This voicing is very powerful, but, being more ponderous than the two-octave pattern, does not lend itself to a rapidly moving melodic line. Otherwise, the same general principles of unison writing apply, and the arranger may freely alternate the two types of unison.

Ex. 92 illustrates a setting of a three-octave unison passage for men's and women's voices alone.

Ex. 92   "Alexander Nevsky"—S. Prokofieff
ⓒ Copyright MCMXLV, MCMXLIX, by LEEDS MUSIC CORPORATION
322 West 48th Street, New York 36, New York
Used by Permission   All Rights Reserved

Ex. 93 illustrates beautifully the practicality of alternating between two-octave unison and three-octave unison and shows how effectively this device solves the problem of extreme melodic range.

Ex. 93   "Ninth Symphony" — L. van Beethoven

Melodic line in alternate voices

This technique is particularly applicable to light, rhythmic materials. It can be described as "breaking up the tune between voices," and is used to achieve a feeling of animation. In faster moving tunes the division might well be in four, or even eight-bar segments. This division will also depend upon the text, which must not be broken up in such a way that the continuity is destroyed.

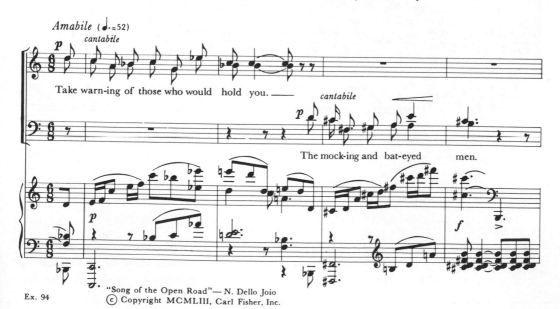

Ex. 94   "Song of the Open Road" — N. Dello Joio
ⓒ Copyright MCMLIII, Carl Fisher, Inc.

This technique may also be applied to "breaking up" a tune among solo voices, a valuable procedure when the text calls for several individually characterized solo lines.

Alternation of unison with harmony

The alternation of unisons with harmony may be advisable when there is need for the voices to indicate the harmonic structure. This alternation should be free and flexible, the length of the unison and harmonized sections being determined by the nature of the musical material. (Review Exs. 86 and 87.)

This technique is particularly valuable when sustained tones alternate with rapidly moving phrases as in Ex. 95. In such passages the sustained tones are harmonized because their duration is sufficient to permit the harmonies to register. The rapidly moving figures are set as unisons because harmonization would tend to obscure both melodic and rhythmic movement. Using this alternation between unison and harmony, the arranger creates an effect of harmonic fullness while at the same time retaining much of the strength and flexibility of the of the unison.

Ex. 95   "A Sea Symphony" — R. Vaughan Williams
© Copyright MCMXVIII, Stainer and Bell, Ltd. Sole American Agent: Galaxy Music Corp.

Because they fail to adequately indicate harmonization, unaccompanied unisons should usually be of short duration. Occasionally they may be strikingly effective when contrasted with fully harmonized sections as in Ex. 96. (See Ex. 213.)

Ex. 96   "Steal Away"—arr. R. Ringwald
          © Copyright MCMXLV, Shawnee Press, Inc.

The unison is not usually recommended when essential character of the music depends upon complex or modulatory harmonies. To convey an understanding of such materials demands a complete indication of harmony. Ex. 97 shows how unimpressive a unison passage can be in a song that is predominantly harmonic in character.

Ex. 97   "You Go To My Head"—H. Gillespie, J. Coots
          © Copyright MCMXXXVIII, Remick Music Corp. Used by permission.

The unison may, however, be employed for materials in which the melody is built on arpeggiation of the harmonic structure, which serves to indicate harmonies, as in Ex. 98.

Ex. 98 "A Dreamer's Holiday"—K. Gannon and M. Wayne
© Copyright MCMXLIX, Skidmore, Music Co., Inc., New York

SUMMARY

Unison writing is one of the most valuable resources available to the arranger. It constitutes an extremely effective setting for strong, flowing, or rhythmic melodies with relatively simple harmonic structures. It is the most natural setting for recitative passages. Using two- and three-octave patterns, it is adaptable for melodic lines in high range. We have seen that interchanging unisons among various groups of voices provides animation, and that alternating unison and harmonized passages provides the effect of harmonic fullness, while retaining the strength and flexibility of the unison. We conclude that unison writing offers great opportunity for the attainment of interest through variety.

Reference and Study Suggestions

1. Find a strong melodic line in standard repertoire (see supplementary examples) and score it for unison voices (S.A.T.B.) with accompaniment. (Generally the treble voice unisons and male voice unisons will be an octave apart.)

2. Use a flowing melodic line such as *Wayfaring Stranger* for a unison S.A.T.B. arrangement with accompaniment. Add interest by shifting the melody to inner voices, a true unison in tenors and altos.

3. Arrange a rhythmic popular tune for accompanied male voices. Resort to two- or three-part writing only at cadences or where some harmony seems a necessary change from the unison.

4. Score *When Johnny Comes Marching Home* for full chorus, principally for unison voices but alternating with four parts at appropriate points. This arrangement may be the basis for a later assignment (Chapter Eighteen) when the accompaniment utilizes an instrumental group.

CHAPTER 7

MULTIPLE-PART WRITING

Voicings with more than four parts may provide a complex harmonic structure and some theoretical problems in chord spellings. Assuming, as we stated in the Introduction, that the arranger has a working knowledge of music theory, the use of more involved harmonies is no real problem. Clarification of any technical point can easily be made by using one of the harmony books referred to in the Bibliography.

Analysis of multiple-part writing will usually reveal a basic simplicity of the harmonic structure; therefore, we are mostly concerned with accepted practices of doubling and voice leading. Before examining the various types of multiple-part writing, we should consider those principles which are particularly applicable to scoring for more than four parts.

General principles

In multiple-part writing, the third in the bass may be doubled in the upper voices if the two thirds are separated by an interval of two octaves.

When inversions of dominant seventh chords are used in multiple-part writing, the bass is not generally doubled in the upper voices. Occasional exceptions are permitted when the bass is the fifth of the chord.

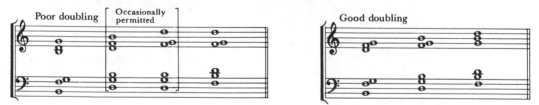

The rules governing inversions of dominant ninth chords in multiple-part writing are essentially the same as those for dominant seventh chords.

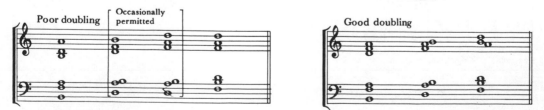

The rules cited previously for dominant seventh and ninth chords apply equally to diminished chords and augmented sixth chords, and are of the utmost importance in scoring multiple-part voicings. Failure to observe these rules is the primary cause of the muddy and thick texture which often characterize the work of inexperienced arrangers in multiple-part writing.

Two considerations regarding the use of consecutive octaves and fifths in multiple-part writing should also be mentioned:

(1) When these intervals represent merely duplication of parts moving consistently in octaves, they are not objectionable, but rather enhance the effect of movement.

Ex. 99

(2) Consecutive fifths may be freely used in the lower voices, where they enhance the sonority of certain passages.

Ex. 100   "Skip To My Lou"—arr. H. Ades

Traditional multiple-part writing

The principles of the traditional style of multiple-part writing are similar to those applying to traditional four-part writing. Here again contrary motion is desirable and the bass line of the harmonic structure is included in the vocal parts. The presence of five or more independent vocal lines, however, presents new problems of tone-doubling. The choice of notes to be doubled is dictated primarily by the demands of good voice leading rather than by an ideal harmonic balance within each passing chord.

Multiple-voice writing is used by contemporary arrangers mainly in combination with other voicings, and with particular types of musical material. Because continued use of traditional multiple-part voicings for long sections easily becomes monotonous, this voicing should be restricted to comparatively short passages. Exceptions to this would be in a very limited area, liturgical music for example, in which stylistic variety might be undesirable. Furthermore, the difficulty of writing for five or more independent parts is often not compensated for by any corresponding gain in effectiveness.

Ex. 101 illustrates traditional five-part setting of a piece of sacred music.

Ex. 101   "Jesu, Priceless Treasure"—J. Bach

Ex. 102 illustrates a contemporary application of traditional multiple-part writing in a passage where the full harmonization requires five parts.

Ex. 102   "There's No Business Like Show Business"—I. Berlin, arr. H. Ades
© Copyright MCMXLVI, Irving Berlin
This arrangement © Copyright MCMLXII, Irving Berlin
Reprinted by Permission of Irving Berlin Music Corporation

Five-part writing with melody doubling

Ex. 103 illustrates doubling the Soprano melody in the Tenor. Note that, except for the doubled melody, this passage represents traditional four-part writing. Melody doubling strengthens the melodic line, adds to the feeling of movement, and results in an effect less rigid than traditional four-part writing.

Ex. 103   "The Unicorn, the Gorgon, and the Manticore" — G. Menotti
ⓒ Copyright MCMLVI, MCMLVII, G. Ricordi & Co., New York
Used by permission of Franco Colombo, Inc., New York

In slightly lower range, Baritones often double the melody, supplementing the four-part writing. In higher range, the Altos may effectively double the melody, other parts distributed as in the following example.

Ex. 104   "The Ten Commandments" — R. Ringwald
ⓒ Copyright MCMLIV, Shawnee Press, Inc.

Parallel motion in multiple parts

Multiple-part writing in parallel motion is used to achieve a combination of movement and harmonic fullness. Harmonization is complete in the vocal parts except for the fundamental bass line which is assigned to the accompaniment. Voice parts move in parallel motion, as is always advisable when movement is the primary consideration. Women's voices are harmonized in three parts with the men duplicating these parts in the lower octave.

Ex. 105   "Prelude" of "1st Choral Symphony" — G. Holst
ⓒ Copyright MCMXXV, Novello & Co., Ltd.

The following example illustrates an adaptation of the above voicing involving more than simple triads. The first three chords again are a trio doubled in the lower octave, but, as the chords become more complex, the voicing is tightened to include the complete harmonic structure. The Basses are omitted entirely in deference to the delicacy of the lyric idea.

Ex. 106   "The Nutcracker Suite" — P. Tchaikovsky, arr. H. Simeone,
ⓒ Copyright MCMXLV, Shawnee Press, Inc.

Ex. 107 illustrates a still more complex musical idea. This formation uses four parts for women, doubled by men. The thickness of this voicing restricts its use to passages in a fairly high register; a lower tessitura would produce an objectionably muddy texture.

Ex. 107   "That Old Black Magic"—H. Arlen, arr. R. Ringwald
© Copyright 1942 Famous Music Corporation

Wide-spread multiple parts

This voicing is used to supply a full, rich harmonic texture for powerful, climactic passages. Here tempo becomes an important consideration, as the pace at which changes of harmony occur must be moderate enough to insure the clear registration of progressions. Where harmonic changes occur rapidly, this voicing would so muddy the texture as to become ludicrous; a simple four-part setting would be greatly preferable. In suitable majestic passages the effect of wide-spread multiple parts is thrilling.

In the first two bars of Ex. 108, the men's voices are scored in four-part writing, Second Alto duplicates first Tenor, and the upper three treble parts mainly reproduce, in the upper octave, the upper men's parts. Similar analysis of other seemingly complex voicings will show that most of them can be reduced to part duplications in various octaves. Bearing this concept in mind will greatly reduce the difficulty of handling this kind of scoring.

Observe that in this voicing the fundamental bass line is included in the vocal parts, while in the examples of writing in parallel motion it is not. This is the primary distinction between the two types of writing, providing to wide-spread part-writing great strength and solidity, less buoyancy and flexibility.

Although the change to contrapuntal movement in the last two bars enhances the effect of this passage, the beginning arranger should bear in mind that the voicing used in the first two bars could have been satisfactorily continued.

Ex. 108   "Song of America" — R. Ringwald
        © Copyright MCMLI, Shawnee Press, Inc.

Ex. 109 illustrates one of many possible variations of this type of scoring. Note the smaller number of parts and the more open spacing of voices, particularly at the first beats of bars 1 and 2, resulting in less thickness of texture and enhancing the feeling of movement. Observe, however, that Bass voices still carry the bass line of the harmonic structure and there is still octave doubling of various parts.

Ex. 109   "Songs of Conquest" — H. McDonald
        © Copyright MCMXXXVII, MCMXXXIX, Elkan-Vogel Co., copyright owners, Philadelphia, Pa

Melody in inner part

This formation is employed only where the predominance of the melody is not a matter of vital concern. In Ex. 110, for instance, the melody has become familiar, having been heard three times previously in the course of the arrangement. In such circumstances the brilliant effect of the high treble parts compensates for partially obscuring the melodic line. Also, the slow tempo permits all the rich harmonic parts to be plainly heard. These are essential conditions for the use of this device. The score should be plainly marked to indicate which part is carrying the melodic line. This will be helpful to the singers in assessing the relative importance of their respective parts, and to the conductor who may wish to redistribute voices on the various parts to strengthen the melodic line. (See Ex. 235-Letter H.)

Ex. 110   "Lazybones"—H. Carmichael, arr. R. Ringwald
© Copyright MCMXXXIII, Southern Music Publishing Company

Scoring the melody in an inner part can be successful in four-part writing, but is more common in complex voicings.

Multiple-part swing harmonization *Parallel motion*

This is the standard voicing for all types of swing tunes. It is scored in either five-part (S.S.A.T.B.) or six (S.S.A.T.B.B or S.S.A.A.T.B.) In five-part scoring, the Bass doubles the Soprano in octaves; in six parts, the Bass moves in tenths with the Sopranos (the top two voices and bottom two voices move in thirds an octave apart). Unless the melody is diatonic, voice leading may become awkward, in which case it is best to alternate this formation with unison or two-part writing. Observe that the Bass voices double the melody and that the fundamental bass line is omitted in the vocal parts for buoyancy and movement.

The bases of this harmonization are the addition of the major sixth to all triads and the use of diminished chords for passing tones.

Ex. 111   "Rockin' Chair"—H. Carmichael, arr. R. Ringwald
Ⓒ Copyright 1929, 1930 by Southern Music Publishing Co., Inc. Copyright renewed 1956 by Carmichael Music Publications, Inc., 119 West 57th Street, New York, New York. All Rights Reserved

Traditional progression

This formation provides a rich texture for swing writing when used with appropriate material. From the performers viewpoint, the relative smoothness of voice leading, resulting from traditional harmonic progression, partially compensates for the added difficulty of the sixth part and the increased harmonic complexity. Observe that, in contrast to the preceding example, the fundamental bass line is included in the vocal parts for greater strength and solidity.

Ex. 112   "It's a Good Day"—P. Lee and D. Barbour, arr. H. Ades
Ⓒ Copyright MCMXLVI, MCMLIV, Michael H. Goldsen, Inc.

This voicing can be particularly useful in broadening out the concluding section of an arrangement. Both this voicing and that described in the preceding section may be used effectively in writing for small groups, with only a single voice on each part. (See Exs. 229, 231B.)

Mixed voicings

The writing which combines all voicing from the simplest to the most complex, with interchange of from one to eight or more parts, is a technique used frequently by professional arrangers. Because of its great flexibility and variety of color, it is a style of writing in which the structure itself is inherently interesting. Moreover, the student will find that it is adaptable to a wide range of musical materials. Such writing, however, requires a well developed sense of balance and proportion and the inexperienced arranger would be well advised to delay experiments with mixed voicings until he has acquired a thorough grasp of the simpler forms. (See Ex. 127.)

Ex. 113   "The Nutcracker Suite"—P. Tschaikovsky, arr. H. Simeone
© Copyright MCMXLVIII, Shawnee Press, Inc.

SUMMARY

This chapter has considered the problems of multiple-voice writing in both the traditional style and with melody doubling. Parallel motion in multiple parts provides buoyance and movement; wide spread multiple-part writing is effective in broad, climactic passages. Other principal considerations can be itemized as (1) scoring the melody in an inner part, (2) multiple-part swing harmonization in parallel motion and in traditional progressions, and (3) mixed voicing, involving use of a variety of voicings.

Reference and Study Suggestions

1. Select several examples of multiple-part writing (see supplementary examples) and analyze for (1) doubling of tones, (2) use of parallel motion, (3) melody in an inner part, and (4) use as sonorities or in climactic passages.

2. Write several extended *Amens* for unaccompanied mixed voices using five, six, and eight parts.

3. Arrange a popular tune in a swing version using five or six parts in any combination you find practical.

CHAPTER 8

SPECIAL TECHNIQUES

THE special techniques discussed in this chapter offer additional means to achieve interest and variety. They include arranging for solo voices with various choral accompaniments, choral pedal points, antiphonal effects, the choral cadenza, and harmonic and melodic alterations.

Choral accompaniment techniques

Solos with choral accompaniment

Effective color contrast can be achieved through scoring passages for solo voice with choral accompaniment within a work scored for full chorus. If adequate solo voices are not available, or if the music suggests fuller tone quality, a group of voices or a complete section may be used on the solo line. Solos requiring a personal, intimate interpretation are not appropriately sung by a group, while other solos actually benefit from sectional reinforcement.

Sustained accompaniment

This type of accompaniment may be either homophonic or contrapuntal and offers a wide dynamic range through use of various neutral vocal sounds — "MM, OO, OH, AH," etc. With these it is possible to achieve a fine crescendo starting with a hum, gradually opening to an "OO," then an "OH," and finally an "AH." The choral background in Ex. 114 is very interesting but the inexperienced arranger may create a satisfactory effect with a much less florid background.

Ex. 114   "Waters Ripple and Flow"—arr. D. Taylor
© Copyright MCMXXVI, J. FISCHER & Bro.

Ex. 115 illustrates another method of scoring similar passages, particularly those of simple character. In this instance the solo line may be sung either by a solo Baritone or by the entire Bass section. Similar passages may be scored in this way for any of the other voices of the chorus.

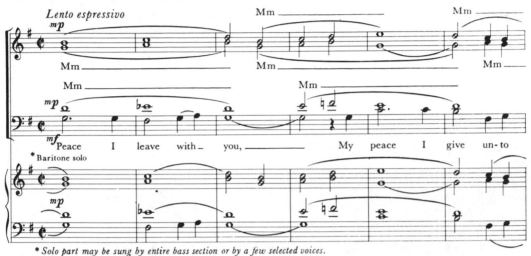

* *Solo part may be sung by entire bass section or by a few selected voices.*
If soloist sings, all other basses should hum the notes of the solo part.

Ex. 115   "Peace I Leave With You"—R. Maxwell & W. Wirges, arr. L. Hoggard
© Copyright MCMXLIII, Richard Maxwell Publications, Inc.

Rhythmic accompaniment

This accompaniment permits a wide variety of syllables other than the one illustrated here, and may include hand clapping, foot stamping or other effects to add rhythmic drive and motion. The variety of rhythm employed is limited only by the ingenuity of the arranger.

(Accompaniment omitted)

Ex. 116   "Song of the Open Road"—A. Malotte, arr. H. Ades
© Copyright 1935 BOURNE, INC. Original Proprietor Irving Berlin, Inc., name changed to BOURNE, INC.
Assigned 1936 to ABC MUSIC CORP. Copyright Renewed
This arrangement © Copyright 1959 ABC MUSIC CORP.
Used by Permission of ABC MUSIC (A Div. of BOURNE CO.)

These accompaniments as in Ex. 116 are often effective as "vamps" preceding the entrance of a solo line.

Arpeggiated accompaniment

This technique is more difficult, both in conception and performance, and requires care in its construction. Observe the careful overlapping of parts to insure the smooth flow of the arpeggiated figuration. This treatment should be attempted only with experienced groups, but provides an interesting style·of accompaniment when used with discretion.

Ex. 117   "Erin Go Bragh" — T. Moore, arr. R. Ringwald
Ⓒ Copyright MCMXLVIII, Shawnee Press, Inc.

Figuration as accompaniment

Choral figurations, reiterated either exactly or imitatively, may be used as accompaniment to a solo voice or section. Again, a wide range of possibilities is available to the imaginative arranger. Ex. 117 illustrates choral figuration used to achieve a rippling effect appropriate to the text.

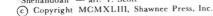

Ex. 118 "Shenandoah" — arr. T. Scott
Ⓒ Copyright MCMXLIII, Shawnee Press, Inc.

Chorus and solo voice

Chorus as answer to solo voice or section

A statement by solo voice or section may be answered chorally as in Ex. 119. This device is easily scored and provides many possibilities for interest and variety.

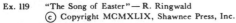

Ex. 119 "The Song of Easter" — R. Ringwald
Ⓒ Copyright MCMXLIX, Shawnee Press, Inc.

Solo voice and chorus together

Certain musical materials or the exigencies of particular situations may suggest the use of the chorus, not as accompaniment to solo voice or section, but as a participant on equal terms. In the first example of this type of scoring, the chorus joins with the soloist in singing a particular phrase, a procedure usually adopted where it seems desirable to reinforce the solo voice for dramatic emphasis.

Ex. 120   "The Creation" *(The Marvellous Work)* — F. Haydn

Though valuable for short passages, this device is not suitable for long sections as the necessity of synchronizing his words with the chorus limits severely the soloist's main contribution — his individuality of phrasing.

Ex. 121 illustrates a more contrapuntal style of writing for solo voice and chorus. Here the chorus sings what might be characterized as harmonized counterpoint, rather than duplicating the melodic line and text of the solo line. Such formations usually require devising a text for the chorus, since the rhythms of the counterpoint probably differ from those of the melodic line. As shown in the example, this text is ordinarily merely an adaptation of the original, duplicating the solo words where possible (See bars 5, 6). Because such scoring does not require precise coordination of enunciation between soloist and chorus, and does not limit the individuality of phrasing of the soloist, it may be continued as long as seems desirable.

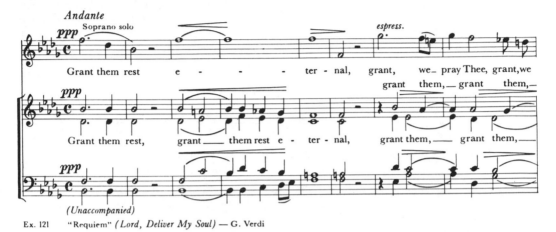

Ex. 121   "Requiem" *(Lord, Deliver My Soul)* — G. Verdi

Use of solo voice for contrast with choral passages

Setting a complete phrase or section for solo voice with instrumental accompaniment may prove useful in extended works to relieve possible monotony of the choral sound. In such compositions, a vocal solo without choral accompaniment may provide the contrast required to give fresh interest to the reappearance of the chorus.

Ex. 122   "Requiem"—J. Brahms

Choral pedal point

Harmonic pedal point

There are several varieties of pedal point. The first illustrated is the harmonic pedal point for Bass voices sustaining tonic and dominant scale degrees. While this pedal point can be useful in writing for any number of parts, it is particularly effective in a passage such as this, which permits the movement of a complete trio in the upper parts while retaining the sonority of the pedal in the bass voices. (See Ex. 41, 71 — in accompaniment.)

Ex. 123   "Holiday Montage"—H. Ades
© Copyright MCMLX, Shawnee Press, Inc.

Rhythmic pedal point

The rhythmic pedal point is a limited form of ostinato, restricted to a single tone or small group of related tones, which through reiteration provides rhythmic impetus. It is usually based upon the tonic or dominant or some combination thereof as in the following example.

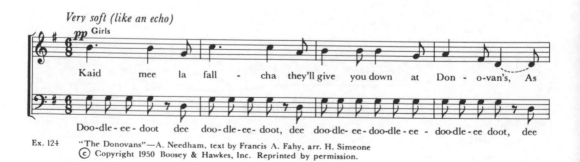

Ex. 124   "The Donovans"—A. Needham, text by Francis A. Fahy, arr. H. Simeone
© Copyright 1950 Boosey & Hawkes, Inc. Reprinted by permission.

Inverted pedal point

Here the pedal point is assigned to the upper voices, either as a section or solo, where it seems to add a sense of tension and excitement.

Ex. 125   "The Roumanian Rhapsody"—G. Enesco, arr. H. Simeone
© Copyright MCMXLIX, Shawnee Press, Inc.

Antiphonal effects

Choral echoing, either exact or imitative, is particularly useful for introductions, interludes, and endings, though it can also be effective at other points in an arrangement.

Following is a fairly complex illustration of this device in a passage of sacred music. Observe the overlapping of phrases resulting from the coincidence of the last notes of each phrase with the first notes of the answer, a frequent, but not invariable practice in writing such antiphonal effects.

Although Ex. 126 is scored in eight parts, effective antiphonal passages can be scored using less complex voicings. (See Exs. 226, 234.)

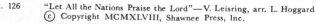

Ex. 126   "Let All the Nations Praise the Lord"—V. Leisring, arr. L. Hoggard
© Copyright MCMXLVIII, Shawnee Press, Inc.

"The Fan"

As is indicated by its name, this technique involves the spreading out and the closing together of vocal lines, as in Ex. 127.

Ex. 127   "Aren't You Glad You're You?"—J. Van Heusen, arr. R. Ringwald
ⓒ Copyright MCMXLV, MCMXLVII, Burke & Van Heusen, Inc.

"The Pyramid"

This involves building choral formations upward or downward through addition of vocal parts. In Ex. 128 a short rhythmic figuration precedes each note in the pyramid. The pyramid here is used to provide a highly dramatic opening for a section of an oratorio. This effect is repeated, with slight alterations later in the section.

Ex. 128   "Elijah"—F. Mendelssohn

Choral cadenza

Cadenzas are sometimes introduced to expand the composition before the final entrance of the principle theme. Used at this point, the cadenza builds anticipation for the return of the theme and insures that its final entrance will have dramatic impact.

Ex. 129 illustrates this technique in a choral setting of a piece originally composed for piano. Observe that the original piano cadenza has been simplified and rhythmically altered to provide voices with singable parts, while the more florid musical elements are retained by the accompanying instruments.

Ex. 129   "A Hymn to Music"—F. Chopin, arr. R. Ringwald
ⓒ Copyright MCMXLVII, Shawnee Press, Inc.

Harmonic and melodic alternation

Harmonic

Introducing fresh harmonizations will often help to achieve color variety and to develop added dramatic interest during repetition of themes. Such treatment must be appropriate to the music, enhancing, not distorting its expressive intent. Ex. 130 illustrates two harmonizations of the same material, the first used as the opening setting of the principal theme and the second showing a different harmonization for its later reappearance.

Ex. 130 "Steal Away"—arr. R. Ringwald
ⓒ Copyright MCMXLV, Shawnee Press, Inc.

Melodic

Alternation of the melodic line is most frequently employed in rhythmic arrangements and is confined largely to familiar materials. Here the arranger may give free rein to his individuality to achieve freshness and originality. The following examples illustrate the application of these principles to a familiar folk tune. The original melody shown first is altered in B to achieve greater rhythmic drive.

Ex. 131 "Comin' Thru the Rye"—arr. H. Simeone
ⓒ Copyright MCMXLVI, Shawnee Press, Inc.

Imitation of natural sounds

There remains for consideration a group of devices calculated to imitate various natural sounds. The following examples indicate some of the possibilities for imitation; many other varieties may be devised by the enterprising arranger.

Ex. 132   "Loch Lomond"—arr. H. Simeone

Ex. 133   "Beyond the Blue Horizon"—R. Whiting and F. Harding, arr. R. Ringwald

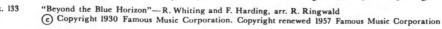 © Copyright 1930 Famous Music Corporation. Copyright renewed 1957 Famous Music Corporation

Ex. 134   "She'll Be Comin' 'Round the Mountain"—arr. H. Ades

Ex. 135   "Around the Corner"—J. Marais, arr. H. Simeone
ⓒ Copyright 1950, 1952, 1962 Frank Music Corporation. All Rights Reserved. Used by permission.

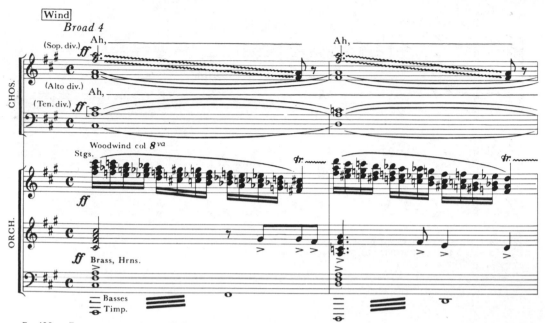

Ex. 136   From an arrangement by R. Ringwald.

Ex. 137   From an arrangement by H. Ades.

Ex. 138   "When Johnny Comes Marching Home"—arr. T. Scott
ⓒ Copyright MCMXLIII, Shawnee Press, Inc.

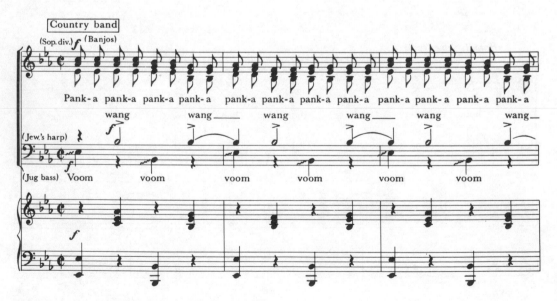

Ex. 139   "Country Style"—J. Van Heusen, arr. H. Simeone
ⓒ Copyright MCMXLVII, Burke and Van Heusen, Inc.

SUMMARY

We know the voice has a capacity for making sudden changes or achieving dramatic effects. When used in choral groups, these vocal qualities can be intensified until it is overwhelming. In this chapter we have given numerous examples of the remarkable ways in which the chorus can become its own accompaniment, imitate sounds, or otherwise provide an unusual background. The use of pedal point and antiphonal writing were illustrated in both traditional and contemporary compositions.

All these devices form a wealth of material from which the arranger can select the most useful for his particular need.

Reference and Study Suggestions

1. Write a sustained humming accompaniment in four or more parts (mixed voices) for a Soprano solo line. In choosing a melody, select a flowing Negro spiritual or a serene folk song.

2. · Use the open fifth on tonic and dominant scale degrees as two different pedal points in the Basses and Baritones. Over these write moving choral parts (on a neutral syllable) to give a feeling of restfulness or a gentle swaying motion. Make only one change from tonic to dominant and return in order to sustain the drone bass effect.

3. By using the one word, "Echo," practice writing antiphonal effects.

4. There are numerous examples in this chapter showing choral imitations of natural sounds. Devise one of your own and write a few measures showing how it would be used.

CHAPTER 9
CONTRAPUNTAL TECHNIQUES

IN the preceding chapters we have discussed the principles of homophonic scoring for voices, in which the writing is primarily "vertical." The importance of individual chord structures was emphasized, while requiring that the connections between them be as smooth as possible. We shall now consider contrapuntal technique, the second main category of vocal scoring, in which the writing is primarily "horizontal." Emphasis is now on the importance of individual vocal lines while requiring that they be harmonically consistent. The horizontal approach to scoring gives each part melodic continuity, individuality and singability, and is therefore highly effective in the choral medium.

Countermelody

This is a technique which offers rich possibilities for interest and variety. Countermelodies may be effectively employed in practically all types of music and in all choral settings with more than one part. The most successful countermelodies are those whose degree of movement varies inversely with that of the melodic line. In Ex. 140, the melody shows considerable movement; its counter is therefore relatively sustained. Conversely, when melodies are sustained, counters should be relatively florid. When melodies contain both moving and sustained segments, counter should move most when the melody is sustained, and remain relatively static when the melody is moving.

A device frequently used to preserve understandability of the text, is to assign to the countermelody a neutral vocal sound, such as "OO, OH, AH" or a hum. The choice of vocal sound will depend upon the character of the musical material and the dynamic level and tone color desired. A quietly expressive passage will suggest the use of a hum, while "OO" gives increased volume and a more rounded tone; "OH" has a more open tone and approaches full volume, and "AH" is the most powerful and best suited to strong, climactic effects.

Ex. 140   "Where in the World" — G. Rowell, F. Waring, and J. Dolph, arr. H. Ades
© Copyright MCMXLVIII, MCMXLIX, Robbins Music Corporation, New York, New York. Used by permission.

Sometimes it is better to use words on the countermelody rather than a neutral vocal sound. As a general rule, this is done late in the arrangement, when the text idea has been well established. At this point, clarity of lyric projection is less essential and may be subordinated to the interest and excitement resulting from the superimposition of two lines of text. Devising texts for countermelodies requires skill and creativity. The lyric idea should be drawn from the basic material and must harmonize with its subject matter and expressive intent. In many cases, as in Ex. 141, the words for the counterpoint will be merely a rhythmic variation of those of the main melody.

Considerable adjustment may be required to fit together the words and music of a countermelody, to make certain that the natural accents of the musical phrases coincide with those of the text. This is skillfully illustrated in the following example. Here male voices duplicate the treble voices an octave lower, an extension of two-part writing. The doubling in octaves of both melody and countermelody strengthens each and produces a distinctively lovely effect.

Ex. 141   "Requiem" —J. Brahms

Ex. 142, in three parts, represents the use of a unison melody for male voices against a countermelody harmonized in two parts for treble voices. Such treatment is common in vigorous, rhythmic music, where moderate harmonic fullness is desired. The melodic line in such formations may be assigned to male or treble voices, and either melody or counter may be harmonized.

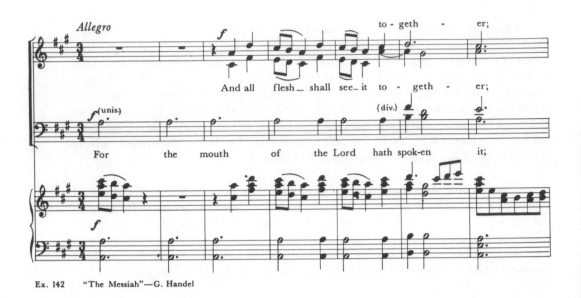

Ex. 142   "The Messiah"—G. Handel

Ex. 143 illustrates contrapuntal writing for two parts in both treble and male voices.

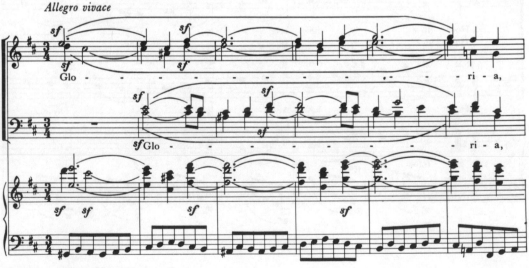

Ex. 143   "Missa Solemnis"—L. van Beethoven

Ex. 144 is another formation in four parts. Here a countermelody harmonized in three parts for treble voices is set against a melodic line for bass voices. In such vigorous, rhythmic materials, the use of words on countermelodies helps provide rhythmic impact.

Ex. 144   "The Burden of Babylon"—G. Bantock
© Copyright MCMXXVIII by Joseph Williams, Limited

In Ex. 145, a countermelody for Basses is set against a melodic line harmonized in five parts for the remaining voices. The punctuated Bass counterpoint contrasts effectively with the sustained character of the melodic line, supplying the rhythmic impetus required to prevent the passage from becoming static. Countermelodies and figurations may frequently perform this rhythmic function in addition to providing contrapuntal interest.

Ex. 145   "Sanctus" (B Minor Mass)—J. S. Bach

The descant

This is a device which is used widely in hymn arrangements, and is useful in all voicings with more than a single part. Ex. 146 illustrates a descant for a passage harmonized in four parts. The descant, originally a florid counterpoint to a cantus firmus, has evolved into a countermelody for a voice or voices above the melody. The general rules for countermelodies apply also to descants — the descant should move where the melody is static and be sustained when the melody moves, although somewhat more over-all movement is common in descants. Descants are often sung on a neutral vowel, as shown in the following illustration.

Ex. 146 "God of Our Father"—G. Warren, arr. L. Gearhart
© Copyright MCMXLIX, Shawnee Press, Inc.

The use of words for the descant is illustrated in Ex. 147. These should coincide with the main text as much as possible.

Ex. 147 "When Christ Was Born of Mary Free"—H. Ades

Figuration

The general principles for writing figurations are similar to those for countermelodies, differing only in that figurations are more fragmentary and less contrapuntal than countermelodies. This characteristic makes them particularly effective with rhythmic music. Figurations are usually introduced at a point where the melodic line is stationary, where they add interest but do not interfere with clarity of melody or text. Either neutral vowels or words may be employed for figurations. In Ex. 148, the words are derived from the main text.

Ex. 148   "My Bonnie Lies Over the Ocean"—arr. H. Ades

Ex. 149 illustrates the use of three-part figuration for Soprano, Alto, and Bass voices with a unison melody for tenors. In this instance, words for the figuration echo the main text.

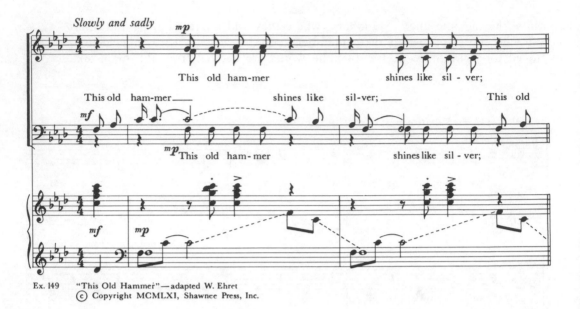

Ex. 149   "This Old Hammer"—adapted W. Ehret
Ⓒ Copyright MCMLXI, Shawnee Press, Inc.

Ostinato

An ostinato is a reiterated figuration which may be basically rhythmic or melodic. Such a figuration frequently appears as counterpoint to a melodic line, particularly in light, rhythmic pieces where the insistence of the reiterated figuration adds drive and impetus. This device is often used as an introductory effect preceding the entrance of the melodic line. In harmonically simple materials, as in Ex. 150, a two-part setting can often prove most effective from the standpoint of rhythmic and lyric clarity.

Ex. 150   "Comin' Thru the Rye"—arr. H. Simeone
Ⓒ Copyright MCMXLVI, Shawnee Press, Inc.

Ex.151 illustrates one of the possibilities available in more complex scoring. The ostinato is harmonized in three parts for male voices against a melodic line harmonized in three parts for treble voices. The insistent repetition of the male voice figuration produces a strong, rhythmic drive.

I hear a voice a - pray- in', pray- in', Lawd,   I hear a voice a - pray - in', Hal - le - lu -

- lu, Hal - le - lu, Hal - le - lu, Hal - le - lu, Hal - lu -

(Vocal parts cued in accompaniment for rehearsal only)

Ex. 151   "I Hear a Voice A-Prayin'"—H. Bright
ⓒ Copyright MCMLV, Shawnee Press, Inc.

Free counterpoint

One of the most interesting and difficult of all forms of contrapuntal writing is that employing free counterpoint. In this type of scoring each voice assumes the role of a relatively independent part in linear motion, its line of direction being determined primarily by melodic rather than harmonic considerations. One result of this melodic concept of writing is that parts can cross freely, (See Ex. 153), making possible the use of wider ranges for the various voices. Parts may drop out and reenter at will, giving to the musical fabric an increased flexibility with fresh impetus at each new entrance. Though one of the more difficult areas of writing, counterpoint offers the greatest possibilities for variety of color and musical interest within each part as well as in the writing as a whole. Ex. 152 is a simple application of free contrapuntal writing.

Ex. 152   "The Song of Christmas"—R. Ringwald
ⓒ Copyright MCMXLVI, Shawnee Press, Inc.

Ex. 153 illustrates the tremendous possibilities for interest and variety available through the more complex application of these techniques.

Ex. 153   "The Seasons"— F. Haydn

Ex. 154 illustrates that this type of scoring is useful in vocal groupings other than four parts. With only three vocal parts, open spacing leaves room for melodic maneuver and obviates the necessity for crossing parts.

Ex. 154   "Messiah"— G. Handel

Canonic and fugal writing

Canonic and fugal devices are among the most interesting and valuable techniques available to the arranger. Presuming a prior knowledge of traditional harmony and counterpoint, the following discussion is restricted to some of the simpler forms of canonic imitation. For more exhaustive analysis the student is urged to consult any of several texts suggested in the Bibliography.

Ex. 155 is a simple illustration of imitation, employing only two parts. Two-part writing can provide one of the most effective media for canonic and imitative styles, particularly in dealing with light, rhythmic musical materials which do not demand rich harmonization. In Ex. 155, the imitation in the second Soprano adds immeasurably to the musical interest as well as emphasizing effectively the rhythmic impetus of the passage.

Ex. 155   "Hymn to St. Cecilia" — B. Britten
© Copyright 1942 by Boosey & Co., Ltd. Reprinted by permission of Boosey & Hawkes, Inc.

Ex. 156 illustrates two-part canonic writing for full chorus. Observe that the accompaniment is subordinate to the choral parts, serving mainly to complete the harmonic structure.

Ex. 156   "Come Let Us Sing" — F. Mendelssohn

Ex. 157-A is an interesting use of two-part canonic writing in octave formation. Since the male vocal parts represent merely an octave duplication of the treble parts, this formation may be regarded as an extension of two-part writing.

Observe that for the same material a full chorus two-part setting without octave formation would be relatively ineffective, as shown in Ex. 157. The two parts are too widely separated, and the Alto voices placed too high. Such considerations frequently suggest the use of octave formations.

Ex. 157   "Credo" *(3rd Mass)* — F. Haydn

Ex. 158 is included to give some indication of the ultimate possibilities of this type of writing using four independent vocal lines.

Ex. 158   "Dona Nobis Pacem" *(Mass in B minor)* — J.S. Bach

SUMMARY

We have examined the various types of countermelodies and descants, emphasizing the relationship of countermelody to melody, and commenting on the use of words and neutral vowels. We have considered the use of figuration and ostinato, pointing up the rhythmic and contrapuntal value of these techniques. Other contrapuntal means such as canonic and fugal writing were also illustrated. The value of these techniques can be better understood when the arranger has experienced the need for variety and a unique quality that only contrapuntal writing can provide.

Reference and Study Suggestions

1. Write descants to several familiar hymn tunes. Use either a neutral syllable or the text.

2. Work out several short passages using any voice combination you wish, accompanied or unaccompanied, illustrating the following:
    a) vocal figurations with a sustained melody
    b) use of an ostinato pattern
    c) imitative writing

3. Try making a two part canon from such melodies as *Down in the Valley*, *Hymn of Thanksgiving*, and *Good King Wenceslas.*

CHAPTER 10
SPECIAL MIXED VOICE GROUPINGS

THERE are two specialized groupings of mixed voices which form the bases for independent choruses, the three-part mixed chorus (S.A.B.) and the two-part mixed chorus (S.B.). These groupings are particularly useful in school groups where a shortage of boys' voices may make S.A.T.B. singing impractical.

S.A.B. writing

This combination of Soprano, Alto and Baritone voices was touched upon briefly in Chapter Four (Review "Three-part Writing" and Exs. 57, 69.) All the resources of unison, two-part, and solo voice writing are, of course, available and should be fully exploited as color variety.

Because of the relative immaturity of the voices in S.A.B. groupings, range limitation is necessary, as indicated on the range chart.

In S.A.B. writing, there are two common types of voicing which assign the melodic line to Sopranos. In one, the Basses carry the fundamental bass line which provides a fairly complete harmony. For that reason extended passages may be scored without accompaniment as in the work from which Ex. 159 is taken.

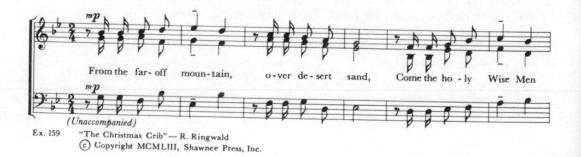

From the far-off moun-tain, o-ver de-sert sand, Come the ho-ly Wise Men

(Unaccompanied)

Ex. 159   "The Christmas Crib" — R. Ringwald
© Copyright MCMLIII, Shawnee Press, Inc.

In the second type of voicing, the fundamental bass line is assigned to the accompaniment and the Basses move with the other voices in parallel or contrary motion. This treatment is particularly appropriate for light and active music.

In Ex. 160, observe the free interchange between open and close voicing as required by range limitations and good voice leading.

Ex. 160   "Little David Play on Your Harp"—arr. H. Ades

In the interest of color variety, the melodic line may occasionally be assigned to the Altos. Observe in Ex. 161 the use of a neutral vowel in both Soprano and Bass parts, a device helpful in maintaining melodic and lyric clarity when the melody is in a lower voice.

Ex. 161   "Hymn to Man"—arr. H. Ades
© Copyright MCMLIX, Shawnee Press, Inc.

Frequent assignment of boys' voices to the melody is suggested, not only for color variety but also to add interest to this part. Ex. 162 illustrates a simple application of this principle, with boys carrying the melodic line against an ostinato for treble voices.

Ex. 162   "Darlin'"—arr. H. Ades
     © Copyright MCMLIX, Shawnee Press, Inc.

Ex. 163 presents more complex contrapuntal scoring for male voices on the melodic line. Although this passage was originally scored for full chorus, its effect is that of an S.A.B. voicing and illustrates the rich possibilities in three-part contrapuntal writing.

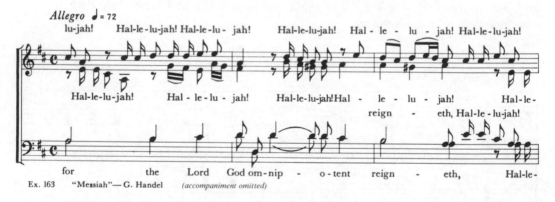

Ex. 163   "Messiah"—G. Handel   *(accompaniment omitted)*

It should be emphasized that all the contrapuntal devices discussed in Chapter Nine are available to S.A.B. writing.

S.B. writing

This voicing is used mainly for inexperienced singers, whose vocal immaturity requires severe range limitations, as illustrated in the following range chart:

All the resources of unison and two-part writing are available to this combination of voices, within the limits of the ability of the performers. (Review Chapter Five "Two-part Writing" and Exs. 73, 78, 85.)

In S.B. writing, the accompaniment must compensate for the thin vocal harmony. Extended unaccompanied passages should be written only to achieve special effects, and these should almost invariably be contrapuntal.

The most common voicing assigns the melodic line to treble voices, with boys' voices treated much the same as Altos in S.A. scoring (See Chapter Eleven). Contrary motion should be used to prevent a continued wide spread between the parts. Ex. 164 applies these principles in a homophonic setting.

Ex. 164   "A Mighty Fortress" — M. Luther, arr. H. Simeone
© Copyright MCMLIV, Shawnee Press, Inc.

The melody line should frequently be assigned to male voices to give this part greater interest and singability as in Ex. 165, an obvious little canonic passage.

Ex. 165   "When the Saints Go Marching In" — arr. H. Ades

Ex. 166 illustrates the effectiveness of contrapuntal writing in two parts for mixed voices. In this instance the composer utilized only Sopranos and Tenors, but the principles of scoring are the same for any desired combination of voices.

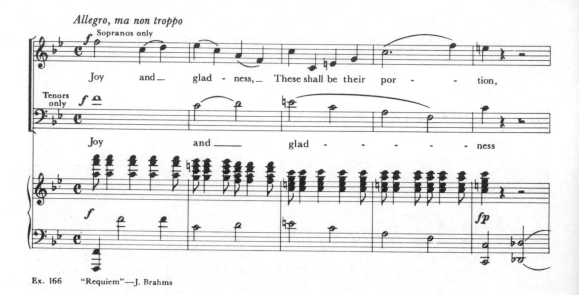

Ex. 166   "Requiem"—J. Brahms

SUMMARY

Although the limitations of S.A.B. and S.B. writing are fairly obvious, the examples have shown that use of these groups is practical. The competent arranger should always have sufficient background to draw on in case vocal requirements demand arrangements of this type.

Reference or Study Suggestions

1. Score Elgar's *Land of Hope and Glory* for mixed voices in three parts (S.A.-B.) using a simple piano accompaniment.

2. Work out an S.A.B. arrangement for a junior high school chorus. Use a traditional marching song and have the boys singing the melody part of the time.

3. Select a sacred song or choral piece and arrange it for an inexperienced choir using just two parts (S.B.).

CHAPTER 11

TREBLE VOICE CHORUSES

TREBLE VOICE groups are found in a wide variety of age groups, from young children's choruses singing only in unison, to adult women's choruses singing the most advanced multiple-part repertory. Each of these groups entails different problems for the arranger. The principal problems are discussed under the headings S.S.A., S.S.A.A., and S.A. writing.

S.S.A. writing

The most familiar combination of treble voices is the three-part chorus made up of girls or women, or of boys with unchanged voices. As discussed in Chapter Three on three-part writing, this voicing is used also in S.A.T.B. scoring for color variety. (See Exs. 90, 94, 95, 100, 101.) The same principles explained in that chapter apply to writing for these groups of treble voices. Also applicable are all the previously discussed resources of unison and two-part writing, as well as those using the solo voice with choral accompaniment. The arranger for S.S.A. groups must likewise remain alert to the possibilities of counter melodies, canonic treatments, and all other types of contrapuntal writing previously discussed. (Review Chapter Nine.)

The range limitations for various S.S.A. groups differ according to the age and experience of the singers, as shown in the range charts which follow. The white notes indicate the limits of ranges for the main body of writing. Possible extensions of these limits for occasional climactic passages, or for a few selected voices, are indicated by black notes.

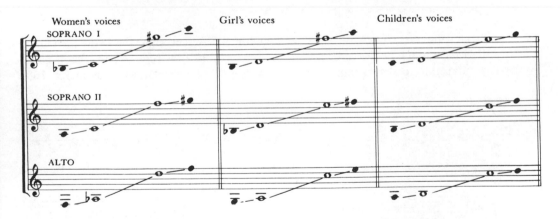

In S.S.A. writing, the melody is usually assigned to the Sopranos. In this case, to make sure the Altos are not forced into an uncomfortably low register, it is wise to choose a key approximately one tone higher than would be normally selected for an S.A.T.B. setting.

In accompanied passages, when it is either impractical or inadvisable for the voices to approximate the bass line, the vocal parts should be regarded as the upper three voices of the harmonic structure; the fourth part is expressed or implied in the accompaniment. (See Exs. 168, 169.)

The rules of part writing and doubling apply to S.S.A. writing, with somewhat greater liberty permitted in the doubling of thirds in first inversions of primary chords. This liberty is acceptable because the marked difference in tone color between vocal parts and accompaniment allows the voices to be heard as a separate identity. When the third is omitted from the vocal parts, an undesirable sense of emptiness may result because of the prominence of open fourths or fifths.

Note that in Ex. 167 the third in the bass line is doubled in the vocal parts on the first beat of Bar 2, and the first beat of Bar 3.

Ex. 167   "Hark, the Herald Angels Sing"—F. Mendelssohn, arr. H. Ades

Despite the choice of a higher key for S.S.A. settings, the Alto part may still occasionally be forced into an uncomfortably low register, in which case, it is advisable to resort temporarily to unison or two-part writing, as in Ex. 168.

Ex. 168   "Red River Valley"—arr. T. Scott
ⓒ Copyright MCMXLIII, Shawnee Press, Inc.

In other cases, it may be preferable to allow the Soprano melody to pass temporarily below the second Soprano part. To insure that the melody will not be obscured, divide the second Sopranos, assigning half to the melody, as in Ex. 169.

Ex. 169 "All in the Golden Afternoon"—S. Fain, arr. H. Simeone
ⓒ Copyright MCMLI, MCMLII, Walt Disney Music Company

At other times, the melody may be shifted temporarily to the second Soprano part as in bar 5 of the Ex. 170. Note the overlapping of the melodic line between the Soprano parts where the interchange occurs, a wise precaution to insure melodic continuity.

Ex. 170 "It's Spring" — C. Boland, arr. R. Ringwald
ⓒ Copyright MCMXLVI, MCMXLVIII, Shawnee Press, Inc.

Crossing of second Soprano and Alto parts is permitted whenever needed to achieve smooth voice leading.

Ex. 171   "Jesus, Joy of My Endeavor"—J.S. Bach, arr. T. Scott
(c) Copyright MCMXLIV, Shawnee Press, Inc.

Keeping the melodic line in second Soprano for long passages is infrequent except where special effects are desired, as in the following example.

*Some voices from other two parts may sing 2nd Soprano in this section.

Ex. 172   "God Rest You Merry, Gentlemen"—arr. H. Hallstrom
(c) Copyright MCMLII, Shawnee Press, Inc.

Assigning the melody to second Sopranos is done more often in swing writing and particularly for swing trios. Here the voicing produces an unusual tone color which is so appropriate for this rhythmic music. For such special purposes, the melody may be retained in the second Soprano part indefinitely.

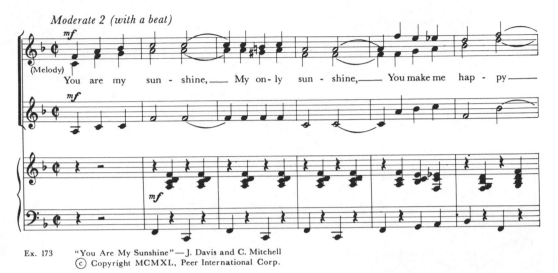

Ex. 173   "You Are My Sunshine" — J. Davis and C. Mitchell
© Copyright MCMXL, Peer International Corp.

Occasionally the melody may be effectively assigned to the Altos, either to achieve color variety or in deference to the character of the musical material. In scoring such passages, several devices serve to prevent the obscuring of the melody. Sopranos may (1) remain tacet, (2) hum or sing neutral vowels, in sustained or figurated formations, as in Ex. 174, or (3) sing contrapuntally against the melody. (See Chapter Nine.)

Ex. 174   "This Is No My Plaid" — arr. T. Scott
© Copyright MCML, Shawnee Press, Inc.

Countermelodies, figurations, canonic devices, and other forms of contrapuntal writing are, of course, useful in S.S.A. writing. Illustrated in Ex. 175 is a simple but charming countermelody for divided Altos against the Sopranos' melodic line.

Ex. 175   "Prince Igor" — A. Borodin
Copyright by Edition Belaieff Sole Agents, Boosey & Hawkes, Inc. Reprinted by permission.

Occasional divisions of any of the three voice parts are permissible for harmonic fullness, particularly at final cadences, as in Ex. 176

Ex. 176   "Lollytoodum" — arr. H. Ades

S.S.A.A. Wwriting

Writing arrangements for S.S.A.A. is in general the same as for S.S.A.; we need be concerned only with the points of difference.

Since S.S.A.A. arrangements will usually be performed by more experienced groups, the range limits are wider, as shown in the Range Chart:

Harmonization in four parts means less dependence upon the accompaniment for completion of the harmonic structure than in S.S.A. writing. Accordingly, there is no limitation to the length of unaccompanied sections. In such passages, the second Alto part will frequently represent an approximation of the bass line of the harmonic structure, though it need not be limited to that function, particularly in contrapuntal writing.

Ex. 177 is a typical four-part setting with second Alto carrying the bass line of the harmony. Observe that a relatively high key is used. This insures that second Altos will not sound strained, and that the texture will not be muddy.

Ex. 177   "Fragen" — J. Brahms

In some material, particularly in popular songs, close swing voicing in four parts may be effective. In such cases, S.S.A.A. scoring is handled as S.A.T.B. writing in this style. (See Chapter One.)

Ex. 178   "Skip To My Lou" —arr. H. Ades

Ex. 179 illustrates a similar usage of close four-part writing in modern serious music. The close harmonization gives to the passage a piquancy which is further enhanced by the sparkling piano accompaniment in very high register.

Ex. 179   "Marionettes" —F. Schmitt
ⓒ Copyright MCMXXXI, Durand & Cie, Paris, copyright owners
Elkan-Vogel Co., Philadelphia, Pa., agents

Ex. 180 illustrates the use of second Alto to carry the melody. Though infrequent, this device is used in materials particularly suited to the alto quality, where it provides a rich color variety.

Ex. 180   "Ah, Bleak and Chill the Wintry Wind" — words by Bates G. Burt, music by Alfred Burt, arr. H. Ades
© Copyright MCMLIV, MCMLVIII, Hollis Music, Inc., New York, New York

S.A. writing

S.A. is the simplest form of scoring for voices, and is governed by the general principles for two-part writing. (See Chapter Five.) All the resources of unison and two-part writing are available with particular emphasis on contrapuntal and canonic devices. In homophonic harmonizations, the principal intervals will be thirds, fifths, sixths, unisons and octaves, though others are permissible to achieve smooth voice leading.

Ranges for S.A. writing depend upon the maturity and experience of the singers. Ranges for three classifications are given in the following chart.

Ex. 181 shows the normal voicing with melody in Soprano.

Ex. 181   "The Seasons" — F. Haydn

Ex. 182 illustrates the assignment of melody to Altos. For melodic and lyric clarity, a neutral vowel is sung by Soprano. This procedure, while not invariable, is frequently effective.

Ex. 182   "Sometimes I Feel Like a Motherless Child" — arr. L. Gearhart
ⓒ Copyright MCMLVI, Shawnee Press, Inc.

Crossing of the parts in S.A. settings is comparatively infrequent but may occasionally prove effective in contrapuntal writing. Because of the relatively limited field of resources available this is a useful device in two-part work. Ex. 183 illustrates part crossing in a simple canonic passage.

Ex. 183   "Flow Gently, Sweet Afton" — arr. F. Cunkle
ⓒ Copyright MCML, Shawnee Press, Inc.

SUMMARY

Considerable space has been given to the ways in which melodic lines can be treated. Herein lies the chief concern of writing for these treble voice combinations. Attention to the details of doubling, crossing of parts, and accompaniments is also important in arranging for such vocal groups. Examine the models carefully as they form the basis on which an arranger can build his own ideas.

Reference and Study Suggestions

1. Complete the arrangement in this chapter of *Hark, the Herald Angels Sing* (Ex. 167), following closely the style of writing which has been established.

2. Select some choral works originally written for treble voices (refer to supplementary examples page XXX) and analyze the techniques which were discussed in this chapter.

3. Try a swing harmonization for S.S.A.A. using either an old popular song or perhaps a show tune which will lend itself to the style.

CHAPTER 12

MALE CHORUSES

MALE choruses may be two-part (T.B.), three-part (T.B.B.), four-part (T.T.B.B.) or more. After a discussion of writing for male chorus in general, the particular problems of each of these main types will be considered.

The resonant quality and rich overtones of male voices in combination present to the arranger both advantages and limitations. Their strength and sonority make the male chorus the most satisfactory of all combinations for unaccompanied writing, and the arranger should take full advantage of this resource. These same qualities, however, limit the use of richer voicings utilizing more than four parts, because of the increased danger of thickness and muddiness of texture. The relatively limited range of the male chorus also presents other problems.

In writing for male choruses, discretion should be exercised in the selection of music, the most suitable being songs that are robust rather than delicate. The choice of inappropriate materials may produce ludicrous results.

T.T.B.B. writing

This grouping is the most common combination of male voices. Since the majority of problems for male choruses arise in passages harmonized in four or more parts, we shall direct our attention primarily to writing in that area.

Ranges in general are the same as those indicated for male voices in S.A.-T.B. scoring, though it is permissible to expand the relatively cramped compass of the T.T.B.B. grouping by extending the range of the Bass voices to include low F. High G is a good note for first Tenors in climactic passages, but should be confined to such purposes.

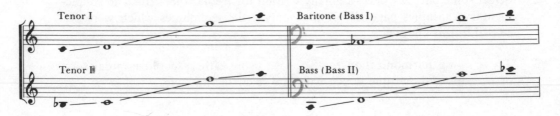

The principles of writing for T.T.B.B. are much the same as those applying for S.A.T.B. scoring except for problems resulting from the differences in range. These will be considered in detail later in this chapter. All the resources of traditional four-part writing are available, as well as techniques applying to parallel motion and swing harmonization.

Melody in various voices

In four-part settings for male voices, the melody is usually assigned to first or second Tenors. In T.T.B.B. writing, as practiced by most of the great composers of the past, the melody is assigned to first Tenors, and this formation is still generally preferred by contemporary composers of serious music.

Ex. 184 illustrates the general pattern of this voicing in traditional style. Although all the rules of traditional part-writing apply, frequent doubling of parts, as on the 3rd beats of bars 1 and 3, is necessitated by the restricted range of the male chorus.

Ex. 184   "In der Ferne"—R. Franz

Ex. 185 illustrates the other voice assignment in which the melody is assigned to second Tenors. This voicing is particularly appropriate for popular music, sentimental songs, school alma mater songs, and, above all, barber shop songs. (The latter will be discussed in greater detail under a separate heading.) This practice is by no means limited to the song types previously listed. It is effective for many different musical ideas, particularly when used in contrast to sections where the melody is assigned to the first Tenors.

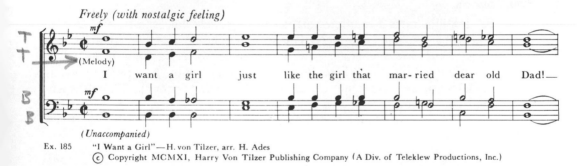

Ex. 185   "I Want a Girl"—H. von Tilzer, arr. H. Ades
(c) Copyright MCMXI, Harry Von Tilzer Publishing Company (A Div. of Teleklew Productions, Inc.)

Occasionally, as in Ex. 186, the melody will be given to Baritones when it maintains a low tessitura.

Ex. 186   "Santa Lucia"—arr. R. Ringwald

For certain melodies, the tone quality of Bass voices is most appropriate because of literary or dramatic associations in the text. Note in Ex. 187 the use of a neutral vowel in the other parts to insure clarity of lyric and melody, a frequent though not invariable practice.

Ex. 187   "Song of the Volga Boatmen" — arr. R. Ringwald
Ⓒ Copyright MCMXL, Shawnee Press, Inc.

Multiple voicing

Ex. 188 illustrates a multiple-part voicing for male voices, a type of scoring which must be employed sparingly. The arranger should take care that the rich overtones, which are a characteristic of the male voices, do not result in an unpleasantly thick texture. Where the melody lies high enough to permit spreading the parts widely, occasional use of multiple voicings provide a highly effective and rich coloration.

Ex. 188   "Die Tagenzeiten"—"Die Nacht"—R. Strauss
Ⓒ Copyright 1928 F.E.C., Leuckart, Leipzig

Use of two- and three-part sections

Whenever limited range of the male chorus precludes continuous four-part harmonization, alternation with three-part, two-part, and unison writing can be effective, as illustrated in Ex. 189. The male vocal quality is so strongly resonant that such scoring approximates the effect of full harmonization.

Ex. 189   "Black is the Color of my True Love's Hair"—arr. H. Ades

Crossing of parts

Where reducing the number of parts is not appropriate, other techniques are available. Crossing of parts is a practical device and the following are examples of this technique. Ex. 190 illustrates the crossing of first and second Tenor parts, a very common practice.

Ex. 190   "Fischerlied"—F. Schubert

Ex. 191 illustrates the equally common crossing of second Tenor and Baritone parts. (See bars 4-6.)

Ex. 191   "In der Ferne"—R. Franz

Ex. 192 shows the extremes to which this technique can be successfully carried when justified by the demands of smooth voice leading. In this instance, the Baritone part passes momentarily above both first and second Tenors.

Ex. 192   "Kantate"— F. Schubert

Shifting melody among parts

Maintaining melodic continuity by crossing parts is useful only when the melody stays within the range of the section to which it is assigned. Where the melody's range exceeds the normal range of any one voice section, it may be broken and assigned to various parts in turn. Make sure this change is of sufficient duration to permit melodic establishment in the new part. In some cases it may be well to suggest that a few "roving voices" with wide ranges be assigned to follow the melody from part to part to insure smooth continuity. Such melodic shifts usually occur between adjacent voices, as in Ex. 193, where the melody goes from first to second Tenors.

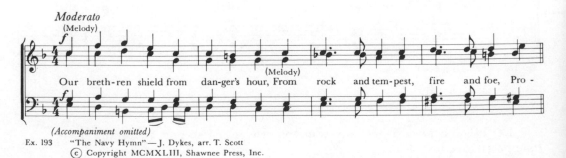

(Accompaniment omitted)
Ex. 193   "The Navy Hymn"—J. Dykes, arr. T. Scott
ⓒ Copyright MCMXLIII, Shawnee Press, Inc.

Ex. 194 shows a similar melodic exchange from second Tenor to Baritone.

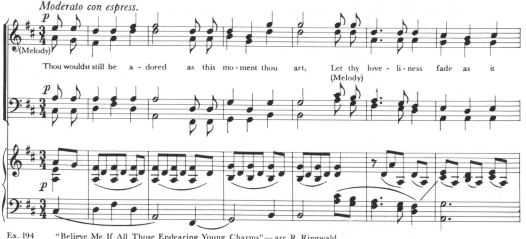

Ex. 194   "Believe Me If All Those Endearing Young Charms" — arr. R. Ringwald
© Copyright MCMXXXIX, Shawnee Press, Inc.

While the above melody interchanges are the most common, unusual circumstances may suggest others. Ex. 195 illustrates shifting the melody from first Tenor to Baritone voices.

Ex. 195   "Black Is the Color of my True Love's Hair" — arr. S. Churchill
© Copyright MCMXLIX, Shawnee Press, Inc.

Ex. 196 illustrates the extremes to which this technique may be carried when circumstances demand it. In this instance, the melody shifts from Bass all the way to first Tenor. Note that the abruptness of the shift is mitigated to some extent·by the temporary duplication of the melodic line in the Bass.

Ex. 196   "Santa Lucia" — arr. R. Ringwald
© Copyright MCMXLII, Shawnee Press, Inc.

Contrapuntal devices

Contrapuntal techniques are extremely effective in T.T.B.B scoring when carefully handled. Ex. 197 illustrates the charming effect of a quiet ostinato for baritone voices.

Ex. 197   "Wehmut" — F. Schubert

Ex. 198 illustrates a more complex but equally effective contrapuntal treatment.

Ex. 198   "Freiwillige herr!" — J. Brahms

Canonic and fugal devices are freely available for this combination of voices and should be fully exploited. (See Chapter Nine.)

The principles governing the use of unison, two-part and three-part writing as color contrast in T.T.B.B. writing are similar to those previously established for S.A.T.B. scoring, and do not require further elaboration. The same is true of passages scored in parallel motion. The arranger should remain continuously aware of the interest and variety available through the use of these techniques.

Barber shop quartets

Recently, there has been a revival of interest in barber shop quartet singing, though not in the art of quartet improvisation which originally accompanied such singing. Now arrangements are scored in "barber shop" and may be sung by quartets or the complete male chorus. There are certain rules for writing in this style: (1) The melody is always assigned to second or "lead" Tenor, as this part is called in barber shop parlance. (2) First Tenors sing the "natural" tenor part above the "lead". The arranger must discover this "natural" tenor part to give his arrangement the spontaneity of improvised quartet singing. On rare occasions, first Tenors may drop momentarily below the "lead" if smooth leading so demands, but this procedure is frowned upon in true barber shop writing. However, the Baritone part may cross freely above the "lead" whenever necessary. (3) The Basses always sing the fundamental bass line of the harmonic structure, a necessary function for them because barber shop singing is always unaccompanied.

The melody may be given temporarily to Baritones when it goes below second Tenor range. In rare instances, Basses may carry the melodic line when words or melody suggest the bass tone quality as in the song "Asleep In the Deep."

The unforgivable sin in barber shop writing is to assign the melody to first Tenors, a practice specifically forbidden by the rules of the S.P.E.B.S.Q.S.A. (the Society for the Preservation and Encouragement of Barber Shop Quartet Singing in America). The sole exceptions to this rule occur in short phrases where the first Tenors may sing the melody in unison with another voice or voices, and in original endings created by the arranger.

In barber shop arranging the harmonic progressions are all important, and rules of part writing and smooth voice leading may be ignored to achieve a richer harmonization. Similarly, rhythmic exactness, expressive quality, lyric continuity and even the melody itself are secondary to the chromatic harmony. Every note of the melody is usually harmonized by at least one chord, and sustained tones are embellished by five or six chords in progressions called "swipes." The progressions most characteristically barber shop are saved for the ending, called the "tag", which should "top" all previous harmonic progressions, before the final resolution to a plain tonic triad.

Ex. 199 is a classic "barber shop" arrangement:

Ex. 199   "Sweet Adeline"—H. Armstrong

T.T.B. or T.B.B. writing

Three-part writing for male voices is used mainly for boys' choruses of high school age. T.T.B. writing is less common than T.B.B. because in most male groups Tenors are fewer than Baritones and Basses. The ranges are:

The principles discussed previously in respect to using passages for color variety in S.A.T.B. scoring, apply to writing for a chorus of this voice combination. (See Chapter Four.) All the resources of unison and two-part writing are, of course, available, and should be fully exploited. As in S.S.A. and other three-part groupings, considerable dependence on the accompaniment is indicated. More extended unaccompanied passages may be written, because using Bass voices on the bass line of the harmony gives the effect of full harmonization. There is less necessity for crossing parts than in T.T.B.B. scoring, because the wider spacing of the three voices allows more room to maneuver without crossing. The technique of shifting the melody among the various parts is useful where the melody does not lie comfortably within the range of one part.

Assignment of melody

There are two main types of voicing for three-part male voices. The most common assigns the melody to first Tenors, and may be accompanied or unaccompanied. Ex. 200 illustrates its use in an unaccompanied selection. In such passages Bass voices usually carry an approximation of the true bass. Either close or open voicing may be used or a combination of the two, as in the following example:

Ex. 200   "Last uns benedein den Herrn" — Lauer
© Copyright MCMXXXIX, Chr. Friedrich Diewig, Berlin - Lichterfelde

In accompanied passages, in which first Tenors carry the melody, close voicing is the more usual form although it may be alternated freely with open

Ex. 201   "La Primavera — O. Respighi
© MCMXXIII, Universal - Edition

voicing in the interest of smooth voice leading. Since the bass line of the harmony is in the accompaniment, it need not be included in the vocal parts which may move freely in parallel or contrary motion, as is appropriate to the musical material. Ex. 201 illustrates such a passage.

The second and less common form of voicing is that in which the melody is assigned to the second Tenors with first Tenors singing a "natural" tenor part. In this formation, the Bass voices do not usually carry the fundamental bass line as this would leave too great a space between Basses and upper parts. For that reason, these formations usually occur only in accompanied passages with the three vocal parts normally moving in parallel or contrary motion, or a combination of the two, as in Ex. 202.

Ex. 202   "I Believe" — E. Drake, I. Graham, J. Shirl, A. Stillman, arr. H. Ades
         © Copyright MCMLII, MCMLIII, Cromwell Music, Inc., New York, New York

Another voicing, less frequent but sometimes effective, is that in which the Basses carry the melody. This device is useful when portions of the melody are uncomfortably low for Tenors. Observe that use of contrapuntal writing insures melodic clarity.

Ex. 203   "The Ballad of Little Musgrave and Lady Barnard" — B. Britten
         © Copyright 1952 Boosey & Co., Ltd. Reprinted by permission of Boosey & Hawkes, Inc.

Contrapuntal devices

All types of contrapuntal treatments, including countermelodies, figurations, ostinati and canonic devices are available to this combination of voices; the arranger should be alert to the possibilities. Ex. 204 shows a simple application of counterpoint.

Ex. 204   "Gesang der Geister über den Wassern" — F. Schubert

T.B. writing

This combination of voices is useful in writing for young or inexperienced groups for whom ranges should be somewhat restricted, as shown in the range chart:

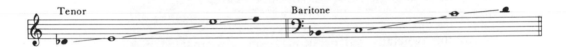

All resources of unison and two-part writing are available (See Chapters Five and Six), as well as all types of contrapuntal scoring. (See Chapter Nine.) Because the accompaniment is needed to complete the harmony, unaccompanied passages should be short and should use mainly contrary motion and contrapuntal treatment.

The most common form of T.B. writing assigns the melody to Tenors and treats the Baritones much as the Altos are handled in S.A. scoring. (See Chapter Eleven.)

Ex. 205 presents a short unaccompanied section combining parallel and contrary motion. Observe that contrary motion helps achieve an effect of fuller harmony. In this type of treatment, the Baritone part frequently approximates the fundamental bass.

To avoid a barren, thinly harmonized setting, Baritones do not usually carry the bass line in accompanied passages. Ex. 206 illustrates an effective T.B. passage, utilizing a combination of parallel and contrary motion.

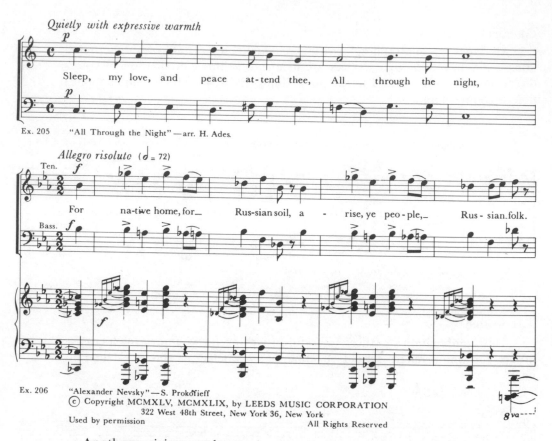

Ex. 205   "All Through the Night"—arr. H. Ades.

Ex. 206   "Alexander Nevsky"—S. Prokofieff
ⓒ Copyright MCMXLV, MCMXLIX, by LEEDS MUSIC CORPORATION
322 West 48th Street, New York 36, New York
Used by permission   All Rights Reserved

Another voicing used occasionally in accompanied passages assigns the melody to Baritones and a "natural" tenor part to Tenors, particularly effective for nostalgic or sentimental songs, as in Ex. 207.

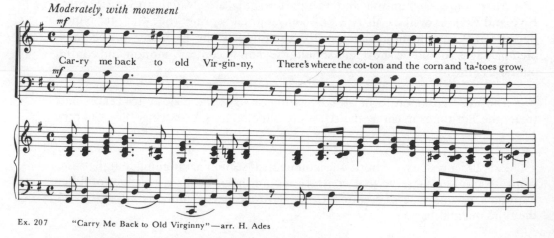

Ex. 207   "Carry Me Back to Old Virginny"—arr. H. Ades

Ex. 208 is a particularly fine illustration of imitative writing for T.B. voices. All other contrapuntal techniques are also available, and the student should be alert to opportunities for their use.

Ex. 208   "Requiem Mass"—W. Mozart

SUMMARY

As in the previous chapter on treble voice writing, suggestions and specific examples which concern the melodic line were considered especially important. The male chorus has an unusual quality which merits the study this chapter has provided. Writing for the barber shop quartet, T.T.B. and T.B. groups were presented in separate sections because of the problems associated with a special style of arranging or combination of voices.

Reference and Study Suggestions

1. Examine some original male chorus material (use the supplementary examples for reference); observe in particular the manner in which the melodic line is treated.

2. Arrange for unaccompanied male voices a strong hymn tune such as *The Navy Hymn* (Ex. 193), or a chorale.

3. Write several short barber shop quartet arrangements.

4. Using a single word, i.e. "Alleluia" or "Gloria," score eight to sixteen measures in a contrapuntal style for unaccompanied T.B.B. (This may be considered an introduction or closing section of a composition.)

CHAPTER 13

KEY AND TEMPO CHANGES

SINCE the impact of key changes can be fully understood only when they are viewed in context, the examples must be studied in their entirety to realize their effect within the structure of the arrangement. Although space limitations do not permit the reproduction here of entire musical works, it is highly recommended that the student obtain copies of the works discussed in this chapter.

The first problem in key relationships is to choose an appropriate one for the first strain. In most cases, the best key will be that which permits the entire melody to be sung comfortably by the Sopranos. A proper key will cause the melody to fall between middle C and E flat, a tenth higher; this range will cover most melodic lines but may be extended by a tone upward or downward, if necessary. This choice of key will prove effective for the simpler settings usually found in the arrangement and also permits subsequent modulation to a higher key.

General principles of key changes

The primary purpose of key changes is to add fresh interest and dramatic impact. This is most often achieved by modulation to higher keys because of the greater brilliance resulting from the higher tonality. The easiest and most natural changes are to closely related keys, such as those of the sub-dominant and dominant, a perfect fourth or perfect fifth higher than the original. Other common upward modulations are to keys a half tone, a whole tone, a minor third, or major third higher than the original.

More rarely it may be desirable to heighten dramatic impact by modulation to a lower key, producing a darker tone color suitable for more sombre passages. The keys most commonly useful for this purpose are those a half tone, whole tone, minor third or major third lower than the original.

Passages effecting a change of key may vary in length from the abrupt leap without modulation to modulations of several measures. While no precise rule can be stated, the common practice is to use extended modulations in arrangements of more serious music of broad scope and stature and shorter modulations and abrupt key changes with lighter materials, particularly when several modulations appear advisable.

Short modulations may be either vocal, instrumental, or a combination of both. For reasons discussed below, extended modulations are either instrumental or a combination of vocal and instrumental elements. (See Ex. 212.)

Modulatory devices

Though an exhaustive discussion of the art of modulation is impractical in this volume, we will present some of the most common devices used in choral writing. For a more general exposition of modulation the student may refer to any standard harmony text.

Pivot chords

One of the most useful devices is the pivot chord, that is, a chord which is common to both keys. Pivot chords may be either diatonic, chromatic, or enharmonic. The following examples illustrate the use of diatonic pivot chords.

Chromatic pivot chords may be used in any of three ways. In A, the pivot chord is diatonic in the first key but chromatically altered in the second. In B, the pivot chord is chromatically altered in the first key but diatonic in the second. In C, the pivot chord is altered in both keys.

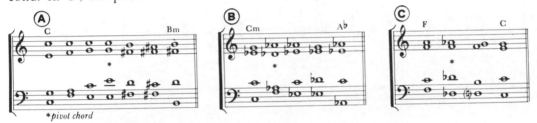

Moduiation may also occur through the use of pivot chords which are enharmonic in either or both keys.

Common tones

Retention in the same voice of tones common to two successive chords is particularly helpful in modulatory passages, as it provides an element of stability and a point of reference for intonation during shifts of tonality. Observe the use of common tones at points of modulation in practically all the examples in this chapter.

Melodic pivot

A third modulatory device is the melodic pivot which is particularly useful in abrupt key changes. In this specific application of the common tone principle, the last melody note in one strain is retained as the first melody note of the next. This can be used only in melodies which do not begin on the first scale step. (See Ex. 210, 216.) Observe that in such abrupt changes of key, the pivot chord immediately becomes the tonic of the new key, rather than acting as a modulatory agent. (See also Ex. 216.)

Unison passages

Another device is use of a unison setting for the passage immediately following a modulation. When suitable to the character of the music, such settings alleviate intonation problems which frequently arise at points of modulation. (See Ex. 215, 216.)

Uses and types of key changes

There are a number of situations which suggest changes of key. The most obvious place is at the beginning of the last chorus or strain of an arrangement. Such a change not only serves the purpose of fresh dramatic impact but also permits a wider harmonic spread for greater brilliance and sonority. This key change is usually in an upward direction, often to the subdominant of the original key.

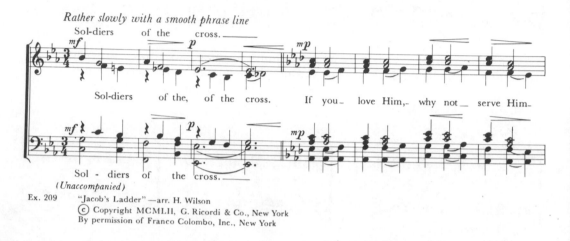

Ex. 209   "Jacob's Ladder" —arr. H. Wilson
ⓒ Copyright MCMLII, G. Ricordi & Co., New York
By permission of Franco Colombo, Inc., New York

The key change to the dominant of the original key is also a smooth, natural harmonic progression. Observe the use of a melody pivot note to provide a sense of harmonic continuity. The melodic leap of an octave at the point of modulation provides a strong feeling of lift.

Ex. 210   "Erin Go Bragh"—T. Moore, arr. R. Ringwald
ⓒ Copyright MCMXLVIII, Shawnee Press, Inc.

Another key change which is frequently employed is to the minor third upward. Ex. 211 illustrates dramatically the sense of lift achieved through a sudden shift of tonality to a key a minor third higher.

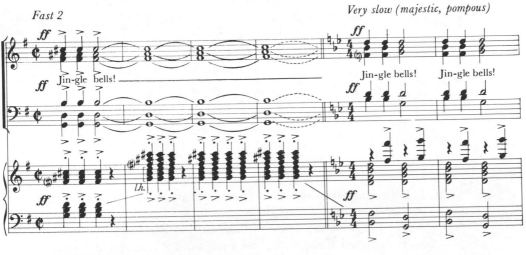

Ex. 211   "Jingle Bells" —J. Pierpont, arr. H. Simeone
ⓒ Copyright MCMLIII, Shawnee Press, Inc.

Another usage of key change is to modulate abruptly up one half tone at each new verse or section of a song. In Ex. 212, only one such modulation is shown, but the same process occurs at the end of each section of the arrangement.

Ex. 212   "Christmas Party" —arr. A. Lewis & J. Platt
ⓒ Copyright MCMLVIII, Plymouth Music Co.

The same procedure may be employed in a series of modulations where the key changes are upward by a whole tone achieved smoothly and easily through the dominant of the new key.

Ex. 213   "Charlottown"—arr. J. Bryan
        © Copyright MCMXLV, J. Fisher & Bro.

Ex. 214 illustrates the type of materials best suited to downward modulation. The half-tone modulation from key of A natural to A flat provides a darker tone for the dramatic quality of the following section. Observe that the modulation is achieved through the use of a unison instrumental passage.

Ex. 214   "The Song of America"—R. Ringwald
        © Copyright MCMLI, Shawnee Press, Inc.

Ex. 215 illustrates an unusual situation in which a downward modulation of a minor third provides a brightened color. The prominence of the A natural in the second strain contrasts effectively with the darker A flat tonic of the first, providing a feeling of increased brightness, despite the downward direction of the modulation.

Observe the use of a unison setting for the bright second strain, which contrasts effectively with the full harmonization of the previous melody. Unison writing is often used in such abrupt changes of key, to ease possible intonation difficulties for the singers.

Ex. 215   "Erin Go Bragh"—T. Moore, arr. R. Ringwald
          © Copyright MCMXLVIII, Shawnee Press, Inc.

Ex. 216 illustrates the use of a downward modulation from C to A flat, to produce a dramatic change in feeling. While the accompaniment gives the effect of modulating a major third downward, the choral parts rise a minor 6th, resulting in a massive spread in the harmonic texture. Note that the tonic of the first key becomes the major third of the second. This use of a melody note as a pivot between keys gives a strong sense of harmonic continuity.

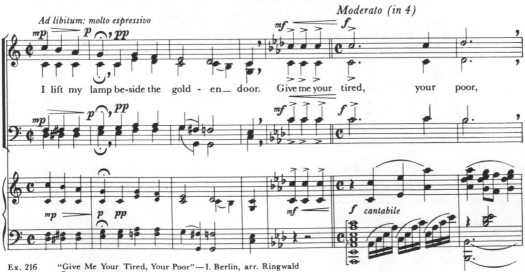

Ex. 216   "Give Me Your Tired, Your Poor"—I. Berlin, arr. Ringwald
          © Copyright MCMXLIX, Irving Berlin
          This arrangement © Copyright MCMXLIX, Irving Berlin
          Reprinted by Permission of Irving Berlin Music Corporation

Because of space limitations, we have been able to demonstrate only short modulations which represent only one variety available to the arranger. Extended modulations built either upon the harmonic progressions presented here or upon others devised by the arranger may be a most effective means of changing key. For two main reasons, however, these more extended modulations are not usually arranged for voices alone: (1) The shifting tonalities are apt to cause intonation problems because singers cannot correctly produce a tone until first hearing it mentally. The chromaticism usually involved in extended modulation makes this mental anticipation of pitches difficult and intonation often is jeopardized. (2) The text is a problem in that either new words must be written for the passage or a neutral syllable must be used. In the first case there is often a lack of textual continuity, in the other lies the danger of an objectionable cliche through too frequent usage.

Extended modulations are usually completely instrumental or are a combination of vocal and instrumental segments. Ex. 217 illustrates the latter combination.

Ex. 217

"Battle Hymn of the Republic"—arr. R. Ringwald © Copyright MCMXLVIII, Shawnee Press, Inc.

The most common key changes to higher keys are up a half tone, a whole tone, a minor third, and a perfect fourth. Downward modulations commonly used are a major third and a perfect fourth.

Modulation chart

The following chart shows basic harmonic progressions which may effectively be employed in short modulations from the key of C to any other major key. These may also be easily adapted for use with the parallel minor keys.

MODULATION CHART

UPWARD   DOWNWARD

Half tone   Half tone

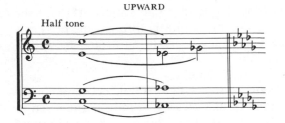

Whole tone   Whole tone

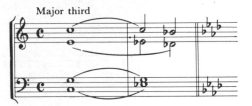

Minor third   Minor third

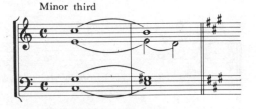

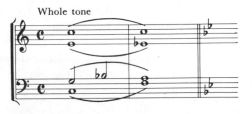

Major third   Major third

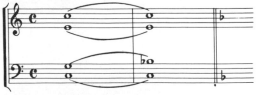
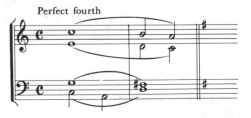

Perfect fourth   Perfect fourth

Augmented fourth   Diminished fifth

Tempo changes

Tempo changes are another valuable device to attain variety. Perhaps the simplest demonstration of the value of this procedure is through the presentation of three settings of a single theme, as they occur in an arrangement of a patriotic song.

In Ⓐ, the melody is set as a strong unison with rhythmic accompaniment in fairly brisk tempo. In Ⓑ, which follows, the melody is fully harmonized in an unaccompanied setting, and the tempo is slow and rubato. The third setting in Ⓒ is again fully harmonized, this time in a maestoso 12/8 meter with a strong rhythmic accompaniment.

In studying these three simple settings, the student should imagine the effect of each, and "hear" the precise impact of each of the changes of voicing and tempo.

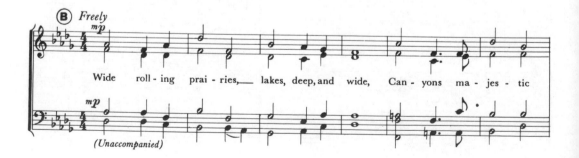

Ex. 218   "America, Our Heritage." — H. Steele, arr. H. Ades
ⓒ Copyright MCMXLIII, MCMXLII, Shawnee Press, Inc.

Another effective tempo change is to double the tempo while halving the time values of the notation. In Ex. 219, Ⓐ proceeds at a tempo approximately half as fast as Ⓑ. A delightful sense of brightness and movement is achieved through this doubling of tempo with its very animated accompaniment. The reverse of this procedure can prove equally effective, that is, halving the tempo so that the choral parts move twice as fast while the accompaniment is sustained.

Ex. 219   "Rockin' Chair"— H. Carmichael, arr. R. Ringwald
© Copyright 1929, 1930 by Southern Music Publishing Co., Inc. Copyright renewed 1956 by Carmichael Music Publications, Inc., 119 West 57th Street., New York, New York. All Rights Reserved

A few moments of careful analysis by the student will result in a better understanding of the values of this technique than would many paragraphs of explanation.

SUMMARY

In summarizing the major points of Chapter Thirteen, the most obvious one has to do with means of modulation. One can quite easily learn the accepted devices as they are catalogued here, but it is the subtle touch and imagination of fine arranging which we strive to teach through comments and examples. Tempo changes occur less frequently than key changes but have great possibilities for adding variety and interest.

Reference and Study Suggestions

1.   Work out a series of modulations for unaccompanied mixed voices based on the devices given in the first part of this chapter. Start and end in the same key; label each device.

2.   By using the modulation chart on page 147, write several extended piano accompaniment modulations as they might appear in an arrangement. Identify each of these with a characteristic accompaniment style as shown in Chapter Three.

CHAPTER 14

INTRODUCTIONS AND ENDINGS

MANY inexperienced arrangers are able to construct the body of an arrangement with reasonable facility but have difficulty in creating a satisfactory beginning or ending. Since many of the principles for writing introductions apply equally to endings, we shall deal primarily with the former.

The basic rule for writing introductions demands that they never assume such importance as to overshadow the main musical material of the arrangement. It is the primary function of the introduction to set the mood and prepare for the presentation of the opening theme, and it must never exceed that function. The success of that presentation must not suffer by comparison with an overly ambitious introduction.

The arranger must carefully examine the material with which he is working to determine its essential character and to calculate the limitations within which to create the introduction. Some materials permit, or even demand, a highly dramatic effect, others require the exercise of considerable restraint to avoid disturbing the mood or distorting the character of the main theme's setting.

Consideration of the introduction should be delayed until the later stages of planning an arrangement, when the arranger will be thoroughly immersed in the character and thematic make-up of the music. The introduction will then be both easier to write and better integrated into the arrangement than if attemped earlier. A figuration or effect from the body of the arrangement, in either voice parts or accompaniment, usually can be developed as an introduction. This is true whether the introduction is derived from thematic material of the arrangement or is original.

Types of introductions

Usually an introduction is desirable to set the mood and, incidentally, to provide a beginning pitch for the singers. It is impossible to catalog completely all the varieties of introductions, but certain types are common enough to warrant description. Familiarity with these will enable the arranger to determine when his music lends itself to a similar treatment.

Introductions may be classified in three general groupings: (1) Solely instrumental (by the accompanying instrument(s), (2) Solely vocal, or (3) a combination of instrumental and vocal. Within each category, introductions may be further classified into those drawn from thematic material or from figuration in the arrangement, originally composed, calls to attention, antiphonal introductions, canonic or imitative, and introductions which are noticeably short.

Although these classifications do not cover all possible varieties of introductions, they serve to indicate a fairly wide variety of common types. Each will be discussed and illustrated.

Introductions drawn from thematic material

Because the presence of thematic material from the arrangement helps to create a sense of unity, an introduction based on this is one of the most desirable. Such introductory thematic material is not always a duplication of that in the arrangement but in many cases represents a variation of a particular motif. Note that in Ex. 220 B the second bar is identical with that of the principal theme, but that the following bars take a slightly different turn. Such melodic variation avoids direct anticipation of the first theme, which would be repetitious and therefore not desirable.

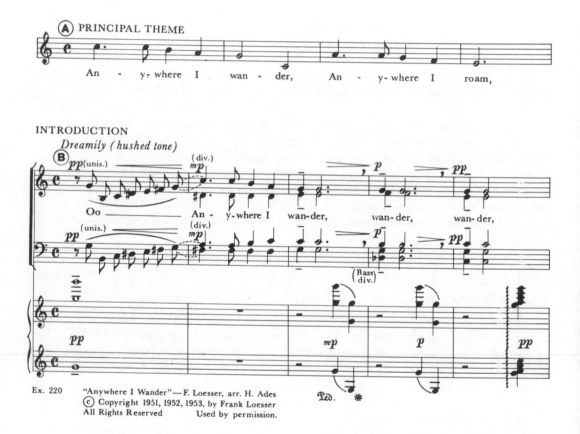

Ex. 220   "Anywhere I Wander"—F. Loesser, arr. H. Ades
© Copyright 1951, 1952, 1953, by Frank Loesser
All Rights Reserved   Used by permission.

Occasionally the introduction may consist of exact restatement of a phrase from the arrangement or composition. Usually such an introduction is scored for piano or other accompanying instruments, and voices are reserved for the full statement of the theme. Ex. 221 illustrates an introduction that is almost an exact restatement of the principal theme except for minor adjustments in keeping with pianistic style. The last bar is altered to provide a progression to the dominant in preparation of the choral statement of the theme.

PRINCIPAL THEME

Ex. 221 "The Seasons" — F. Haydn

Introductions drawn from figuration or effect in arrangement

A common procedure, which may take several forms is to use a figuration, arpeggiated pattern or some other effect. Ex. 222 illustrates a simple application of this principal in which the figuration employed is the basis, not only for the introduction, but for the accompaniment of an entire section of the mass. The student will profit from careful analysis of this accompaniment. (See also Ex. 49.)

Ex. 222 "Mass in B Minor" — J.S. Bach

The use of an ostinato effect for setting the opening theme of a rhythmic arrangement may well suggest its employment as an introduction. (See Ex. 150.)

Original material setting mood

Introductions not drawn from thematic material require greater skill to establish continuity of mood and character with the music to follow. In Ex. 223, the use of a neutral vowel on a harmonized passage in minor tonality beautifully prepares for the presentation of the tragic subject matter of the theme.

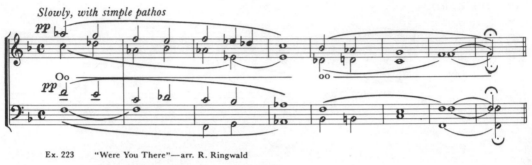

Ex. 223   "Were You There"—arr. R. Ringwald
© Copyright MCMXLIV, Shawnee Press, Inc.

In Ex. 224, the piano alone effectively establishes a mood of entirely different character.

Ex. 224   "Ezekiel Saw the Wheel" —arr. H. Simeone
© Copyright MCML, Shawnee Press, Inc.

Antiphonal introductions

Ex. 225 illustrates an introduction using an antiphonal effect to create a sense of wonderment, beautifully in keeping with the character of the song.

Ex. 225   "Alice in Wonderland" — S. Fain, arr. H. Simeone
ⓒ Copyright MCML, MCMLI, Walt Disney Music Company

Calls to attention

Certain types of introductions serve mainly as fanfares and use dramatic effects to announce the coming of the main body of the work. Such introductions, as in Ex. 226, may be characterized as calls to attention.

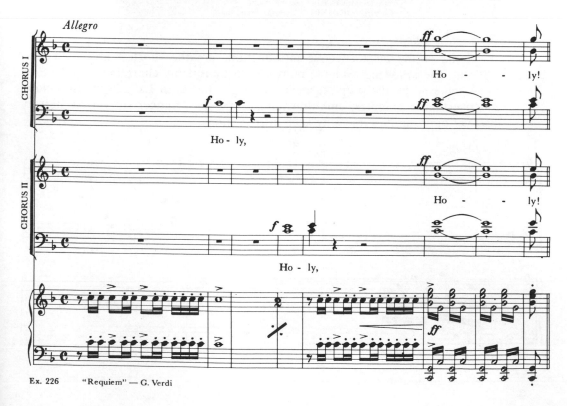

Ex. 226   "Requiem" — G. Verdi

Canonic or imitative introductions

Canonic effects and imitation can also be highly effective devices in introductions. Ex. 227 represents a rather extended use of both techniques to establish the roistering spirit of the traditional wassail song.

Ex. 227   "Gloucestershire Wassail"—arr. T. Scott
ⓒ Copyright MCMXLIV, Shawnee Press, Inc.

Short introductions

Some of the most effective introductions are the shortest and least pretentious. The following example represents a thoroughly charming introductory effect achieved by the simplest means. A beginning as in Ex. 228 is often more effective than a complex, ambitious effort, and the arranger should be alert to discover opportunities for using such introductions.

Ex. 228   "Miracles of Faith"—D. Milhaud
ⓒ Copyright MCMLIII, G. Schirmer, Inc.

Types of endings

Most of the principles governing writing of introductions apply also to ending. There are, however, certain types of endings which warrant special consideration.

Repetition of final phrase

One of the simplest and most common devices is to repeat the final phrase once or more, using a false cadence until the fiinal resolution. Ex. 229 illustrates how this technique is used to end a bright, rhythmic number.

Ex. 229 "Hoop Dee Doo" — F. Loesser, arr. H. Ades
ⓒ Copyright 1950 by Frank Music Corp.
All Rights Reserved   Used by permission

Ex. 230 illustrates canonic imitation used in an ending which gradually fades to a quiet finish.

Ex. 230   "Peer Gynt Suite"—E. Grieg, arr. H. Simeone
ⓒ Copyright MCMLXIII, Shawnee Press, Inc.

Stretching of final phrase

Another very common practice is to stretch the final phrase by doubling or quadrupling the note values, thus writing out a broadening of tempo in the ending of the arrangement. This device is often used along with alternation of the melodic line. In Ex. 231 the note values of the original phrase have been quadrupled.

ORIGINAL THEME

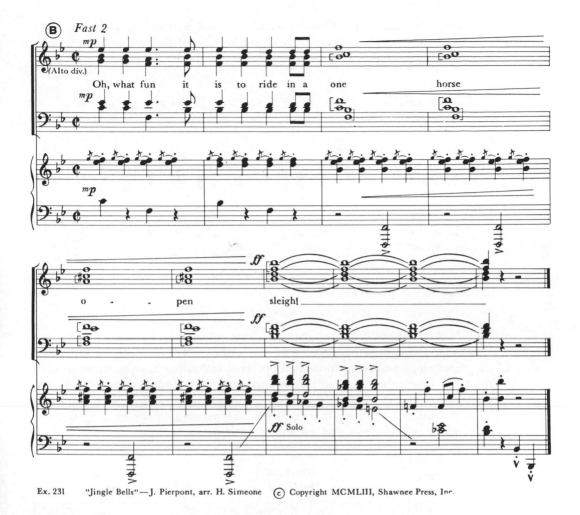

Ex. 231   "Jingle Bells"—J. Pierpont, arr. H. Simeone © Copyright MCMLIII, Shawnee Press, Inc.

Additional material following final phrase

In this treatment the final phrase is presented in unaltered form up to

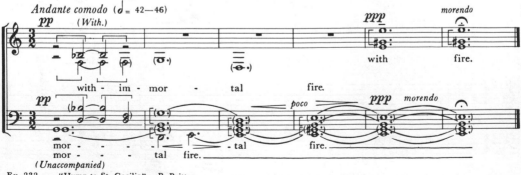

Ex. 232   "Hymn to St. Cecilia"—B. Britten
© Copyright 1942 by Boosey & Co., Ltd. Reprinted by permission of Boosey & Hawkes, Inc.

or including the last note, following which original material is added to bring the arrangement to a close. The simplest application of this technique involving only the addition of two soft chords is illustrated in Ex. 232.

Ex. 233 shows an extended application of the same principle.

Ex. 233   "America, the Beautiful" — S. Ward, arr. R. Ringwald
© Copyright MCMLI, Shawnee Press, Inc.

Repetition of introductory effect

Another frequently used device utilizes either exact or imitative repetition of the effect employed in the introduction. This technique has the virtue of contributing to a sense of unity in the arrangement. The ending illustrated in Ex. 234 is taken from the same arrangement discussed in Ex. 225. It is recommended that the student examine this complete arrangement in order to gauge the impact of its introduction and ending.

Ex. 234   "Alice in Wonderland" — B. Hilliard, S. Fain, arr. H. Simeone
© Copyright MCML, MCMLI, Walt Disney Music Company

SUMMARY

A detailed classification of introductions and endings has been given to show the extent to which an arranger may go in drawing on material. It is well to repeat in the summary that these sections are better left until the arrangement has taken a form and character which can properly be represented in these critical places.

Reference and Study Suggestions

1. Make a detailed study of several introductions from each category given in the supplementary material in the Appendix. Find examples of your own for further analysis.

2. For any voice and accompaniment combination you wish, using a neutral syllable and your own melodic ideas, score the following introductions:
   a) set the mood for a lullaby
   b) a dramatic fanfare
   c) antiphonal effects

3. Using *Jingle Bells* (Ex. 231) as a model, extend the final phrase of the first stanza of *America the Beautiful* ("From sea to shining sea.") for accompanied S.A.T.B.

CHAPTER 15

RESOURCES IN COMBINATION

HAVING examined and analyzed techniques for choral arranging, we now consider combining these resources. To do this effectively depends on the arranger's ability to develop a feeling for structural balance and a sensitivity to the relationships of his many resources.

One basic principle governs the form and structure of an arrangement — it should begin simply and grow in relative complexity as it develops. The presentation of a new musical idea is usually sufficient to hold interest at the beginning, but as the music progresses, and the themes reappear, it takes great ingenuity to hold an arrangement together. Interest must be maintained in an increasing degree until the climax is reached, usually the concluding section. In some cases, the climax occurs earlier in the work and the remainder of the arrangement tapers off to a quiet conclusion. In either case the basic principle remains.

As an illustration of skillful use of combined resources, a complete arrangement is given in this chapter. The accompanying analysis points out the use of many of the techniques and devices discussed earlier. Here is an impressive corroboration of the contention that the most effective results in choral arranging can be achieved through the simplest of means.

Introduction

Ex. 235   "Battle Hymn of the Republic" — W. Steffe, arr. R. Ringwald
Ⓒ Copyright MCMXLIII, Shawnee Press, Inc.

Introduction

This is a highly effective instrumental "call to attention" employing drum and bugle call effects. Note the motivic derivation from the theme.

Letter A

Bars 1 — 8: Unison voices on the theme at a low dynamic level against a continuation of the drum and bugle accompaniment begin the arrangement with simplicity and strength.

Letter B

Bars 1 — 8: continue in the same vein, with increasing power as dynamic level is gradually raised. The accompaniment figurations become more active.

Letter C

Bars 1 — 8: Statement of second theme in a five-part setting with Baritones strengthening melody in lower octave. Observe that without this Baritone part, this passage would be simple four-part writing. The accompaniment continues to gain momentum as the arrangement increases in complexity.

Letter D

Bars 1 — 2: Voices join in the drum-like accompaniment as "vamp" marching effect preparing second entrance of opening theme. Bars 3 — 10: Baritone solo over continuing rhythmic accompaniment acts as a setting for second appearance of opening theme. A "piccolo" counter melody appears in the accompaniment, making three musical ideas in progress at this point. Note again the building complexity.

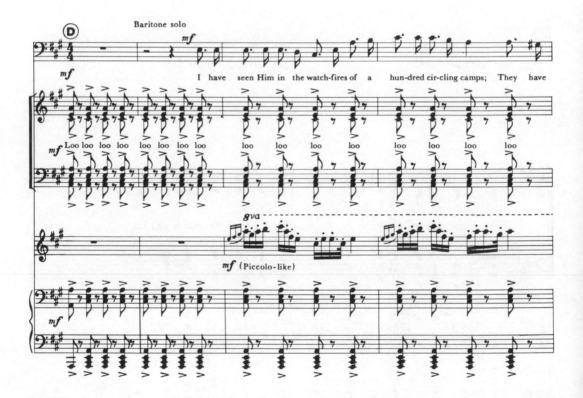

build - ed Him an al - tar in the eve - ning dews and damps; I can read His right-eous sen-tence by the

loo loo loo loo loo loo loo loo loo loo loo loo

dim and flar-ing lamps, His day is march - ing on. _____

loo loo loo loo loo loo loo loo loo loo loo lo loo

Letter E

Bars 1 — 6: Here is the second appearance of the second theme, four-part writing in parallel motion for added movement. Basses double melody while the fundamental bass is assigned to the accompaniment. A triplet figure in the accompaniment enhances the feeling of building. Bars 7 — 8: Traditional four-part harmonization closes the phrase strongly.

Letter F

Bars 1 — 4: A broadening instrumental and vocal modulation adds to the sense of anticipation. The vocal writing uses a simple four-part open voicing on a neutral syllable.

Letter G

Bars 1 — 5: The third appearance of opening theme in a very expressive rubato section uses two-part writing for treble voices doubled by the male voices in the lower octave. Against a drum roll accompaniment, this change to an ad lib tempo from the preceding strong rhythmic sections is effective not only as contrast but also enhances the growing expectation of the climax. Bars 6 — 8: Again four-part traditional harmonization is used to close the phrase.

Letter H

Bars 1 — 4: This third appearance of the second theme is the climax of the arrangement. Voices are in multiple parts with the melody in an inner voice. The accompanying figure strongly scored in octaves adds to the excitement of this climactic passage. In bars 5 — 8 the climax is past, the arrangement decreases in complexity as it moves toward the ending, using four-part writing and a simpler accompaniment. Bars 9 — 10: The ending "Amen" uses wide-spread multiple-part voicing and a broadening triplet figure in the accompaniment, concluded by a return to the drum motif.

With the exception of the four-bar passage at its climax, this arrangement uses only simple devices of choral writing, making it accessible to a wide range of choral groups.

SUMMARY

The conclusions drawn from an analysis of the extended arrangement of *Battle Hymn of the Republic* should primarily be, (1) the practical means by which the arranger has accomplished his purpose, and (2) the excellent total choral effect that has been achieved.

Reference and Study Suggestions

1. From your own library of choral music, chose two larger choral arrangements and analyze them for devices and techniques. Observe specifically the point of climax and how it was accomplished.

2. Find several compositions or tunes which you feel will lend themselves to extended arrangements and itemize techniques that might be adapted to each. This is the basis for study assignments in the following two chapters.

CHAPTER 16

PLANNING ARRANGEMENTS

WHEN the choral arranger has acquired skill and restraint in combining resources, he should then understand the procedures for planning and scoring arrangements. This chapter deals with the former by showing two main steps of preparation followed by a method which emphasizes the importance of good planning.

Step one

The initial step should be the careful consideration of the type of group for which the arrangement is to be written and the circumstances under which it is likely to be performed. In writing for young or inexperienced groups in school situations, for instance, there must be taken into account certain limitations characteristic of youthful and untrained voices. In such groups the vocal quality in the higher register tends to become thin and harsh while the lowest registers are relatively weak and unfocused. For that reason, the range employed must be somewhat restricted. (See index for range charts.) Similar conservatism must be employed in the scoring. For such groups, the more complex voicings present such performance difficulties that they should be avoided. A simple effect well performed will always prove more effective than a complex one inadequately rendered.

Particular attention must be given to the smoothness of voice leading. Awkward and difficult intervals must be avoided and unusual harmonic progressions minimized. Chromatic and dissonant writing should be used sparingly.

The arranger should become as familiar as possible with the vocal capabilities of the individual singers in order to be fully aware of the limitations under which he must operate. Such intimate knowledge of their vocal capabilities will also enable him to take advantage of any unusual ability in one section or another which might help to mitigate the severity of these limitations. The presence of one or more voices of solo calibre can be immensely helpful in attaining variety through the scoring of passages for solo voice with choral accompaniment. Also, the arranger should ascertain the availability of instrumental soloists or groupings of instrumentalists. Through judicious use of such auxiliaries, he may be able to brighten and vary his arrangements without increasing the complexity of choral writing. (See Chapter Eighteen: Chorus With Instrumental Groups.)

Writing arrangements for experienced or professional choruses presents problems of a different nature; these vary according to the circumstances under which the arrangements are to be performed. The media which allow the arranger the grestest flexiblity and latitude are radio and recordings. Here the chorus may be closely grouped for a solid, compact body of sound, and microphones placed to catch every subtle inflection of scoring or interpretation. The most complex voicings may be so perfectly balanced that their exact reproduction becomes a theoretical possibility. The realization of this depends largely upon the skill of the radio or recording engineer. Whenever possible the arranger should be present in the control room during rehearsals and performances. If this is impractical, he should mark a score for the engineer and give him instructions as to the precise effects desired in each section of the arrangement.

The concert hall offers problems that are similar in some respects but quite different in others. Here too the chorus may be compactly grouped for solidity of sound, but unless the acoustical conditions are perfect, the effects employed must be of somewhat broader character. In most auditoriums, sound projected by the chorus tends to become diffuse and fine subtleties and complexities of intricate scoring are lost. This limitation is more than compensated by the excitement gained in hearing in live performance the actual tone quality of voices, undistorted by electronic reproduction. The concert hall has the additional advantage that choral balance and dynamic level are no longer dependent upon microphone placement or the discretion of the radio or recording engineer.

Writing for the theatre presents somewhat different problems. The choral group for the average theatrical production is relatively small, limiting considerably the number of parts into which the chorus can be successfully divided. Furthermore, the exigencies of staging frequently require that singers be widely separated from each other so there is less opportunity of choral grouping which permits subtle effects or complex voicings. It is advisable that most scoring for the theatre be along the broadest possible lines, using unison or two parts. The arranger should work closely with the producer or stage director and determine the points at which the chorus will be most widely dispersed and limit his vocal writing accordingly. It is always best to err on the side of caution in scoring. Even when advance planning indicates a compact grouping for the chorus, all too frequently the director will alter the plans for stage groupings. The arranger who has counted on compact grouping of his singers may find them scattered about the stage with most unfortunate effects upon his carefully and subtly conceived arrangement.

The situation in television is much like that in the theatre except that it is more frequently possible to determine in advance those points at which the chorus may be compactly grouped and have access to microphones. At such times the arranger may write with the same freedom as for radio and recording. At other times singers may be as widely dispersed as in the theatre with the additional disadvantage that it is a practical impossibility to have microphones everywhere at once. Situations of this type call for scoring in unison or two parts to achieve a satisfactory sound.

Summarizing briefly the first step, the arranger is vitally concerned with many aspects of the performance of his writing. He must become thoroughly familiar with the possibilities and limitations of the particular group with which he is working; he must take into careful account the factors peculiar to the media in which his arrangements are to be performed.

Step two

The second step should be a careful study of the materials which are to be used. This study involves equal attention to the music and the text until there is a thorough understanding of the basic character and expressive intent of the music.

The approximate dimensions of the arrangement should now be determined; the character of the musical material will indicate the extent of treatment which is appropriate. A decision should be reached as to how many sections should be included and in what order — should both verse and chorus be used, how many verses, etc. Themes for the opening and closing sections of the arrangement should also be chosen at this time.

The considerations that operate to expand or limit the scope of the arrangement are the number of verses available and the number of musical themes. If there are many verses, especially the narrative type which easily maintain interest, the arrangement may be fairly lengthy. If there is only a single verse, the monotony inherent in excessive repetitions will limit considerably the length of the arrangement. The same principle applies to the number of musical themes available, though greater variety through treatment is available here.

The sketch plan

Following this preliminary study, the arranger should undertake to outline the structure of the arrangement before scoring a single note. This outlining is usually accomplished most effectively through the preparation of a sketch of the complete arrangement.

There are a number of purposes served by the sketch plan but perhaps the most important is its contribution to achieving that sense of form and development discussed previously. By making sketches of a number of possible treatments of various themes, the arranger can study and organize these to gain the most effective contrasts, and create the development from simplicity to relative complexity needed to sustain interest and build toward a climax.

Without this study and organization of sketched ideas, the arranger may unhappily discover in the later stages of work that an idea has been used in an early section which might better have been reserved until later. Then, either the arrangement must be almost completely rescored, or a less effective idea substituted. As a result the arrangement will lack the dramatic impact which it might have had.

The sketch does not represent every note which is to appear in the finished arrangement. Rather, show only the first bar or two to indicate the vocal and accompaniment styles for that section. The remainder of each section should be outlined roughly and filled in when the arrangement is scored.

As previously discussed, the introduction should not usually be sketched until the body of the arrangement has been planned. The sketch should begin with a setting for the first statement of the principal theme. At this point the arranger should not wait hopefully for a sudden stroke of inspiration. Inspiration is a highly unpredictable attribute and its unassisted arrival may be long delayed. He must arouse and stimulate his imagination by raising questions as to the character and possibilities of treatment of the musical material with which he is working. Below is a series of possible questions which might well be raised concerning various aspects of the arrangement. These, and others which will suggest themselves, should prove helpful in focusing the attention on a flow of creative ideas.

Setting for principal theme

1. Does the theme have a strong expressive character for which an unaccompanied setting would be appropriate, or does greater emphasis upon rhythmic movement suggest an accompaniment?

2. Is it a strong, flowing, or rhythmic melodic line with simple harmonies which would lend itself well to a unison treatment?

3. Does it lie naturally in thirds, sixths or horn-call patterns which might suggest a two-part setting?

4. Is the harmonic structure fairly complex, and is the tempo sufficiently moderate to require a four-part setting?

5. Is there a natural countermelody or contrapuntal line suggested by the harmonic structure, or can one be devised?

6. Are there natural open spaces in the melody requiring figuration?

7. Has the theme the vigorously rhythmic character which might suggest an ostinato?

Secondary themes should be similarly tested for character and possibilities of treatment which will contrast agreeably with the opening statement of the principal theme. The arranger should bear in mind that the first statements of themes should be relatively simple; more complex or unusual treatments are best reserved for a reappearance of the themes.

Settings for reappearance of themes

1. Does the theme lend itself to solo treatment with harmonized, rhythmic, or arpeggiated accompaniment?

2. Can a fresh harmonization be devised which will remain consistent with the character of the musical material?

3. Are there suitable opportunities for more elaborate contrapuntal treatments, canonic, or fugal devices?

4. Can the theme be set effectively with the melody in an inner part?

5 Are there phrases suggesting imitation or antiphonal effects?

6. Is a change of key indicated either for dramatic effect or to permit the voices to be wider spread for a change of color?

7. Would a change of tempo for interest and variety be in character with the musical material?

These and other questions should stimulate a flow of ideas which should be sketched to show a number of possible treatments for the various themes. The arranger must now attempt to balance and contrast these according to the basic principle which has been previously suggested. — from simplicity through relative complexity toward a climax.

In the attempt to achieve variety and interest the arranger is cautioned against introducing changes of color so frequently as to produce a disjointed effect, and causing his various treatments to appear fragmentary. Each treatment should be continued long enough to become well established and have a significant musical effect. The required length in slow tempos is four to eight bars; in faster tempos eight to sixteen bars should be written in one type of voicing before a change of color is attempted.

Good taste and restraint on the part of the arranger are necessary to achieve a happy balance between various contrasting but stylistically integrated segments. Without these attributes, an arrangement may become a hodge-podge of totally unrelated effects contrasted so violently that the result is a stylistic monstrosity. The arranger is urged to err on the side of caution until he has developed a sense of balance and proportion in combining the many varied resources available.

Having completed the sketching of the body of the arrangement, the arranger should now turn to the introduction, modulations if any, and the ending, letting these grow naturally from the material already sketched.

On superficial examination it might appear that using the sketch plan is more laborious and time-consuming than proceeding directly with scoring, but such is not the case. Scoring proceeds far more rapidly when a sketch has been previously prepared, and ideas flow much more freely during the flexible process of sketching than within the confines and limitations of the creation of a final score. Sketching permits concentration upon the broad outlines of the arrangement rather than upon technical detail and results in the production of better organized arrangements with a minimum expenditure of time and energy.

The sketch now complete, scoring may begin. The arranger's task is nine-tenths finished. All that remains is to transfer the sketch to score paper, refining and improving as the work proceeds. At this point another great advantage of the sketch plan emerges. All the ideas developed during the production of the sketch have been germinating in the mind of the arranger, and as he returns to them, many refinements and improvements will suggest themselves to give the work that final polish which characterizes effective arrangements.

SUMMARY

If he does not have some well though out procedures, the arranger is likely to fall into bad habits because he is without a plan. Chapter Sixteen presents a systematic manner of approaching this problem. The questions regarding thematic development and continuity should be helpful until one has attained sufficient discipline to control these elements in arranging.

Reference and Study Suggestions

Following a plan as outlined in this chapter, sketch in some detail two of the compositions you selected for study at the conclusion of Chapter Fifteen. This is the basis for a study assignment in the following chapter on scoring arrangements.

CHAPTER 17

SCORING ARRANGEMENTS

THE student is now ready to proceed with the actual scoring of his arrangement. Materials needed are staff paper and soft lead pencils. Manuscript paper on which there are twelve staves is probably the best as it will accommodate two six-staff systems (mixed voices) for full scoring or three four-staff systems for condensed scoring. There are many sizes and types of staff paper available, so select that which suits the particular vocal and instrumental combination you are using. Writing with pencil instead of ink permits corrections and improvements to be made easily as the work progresses.

Full scoring

In the full score, a separate staff is assigned to each voice part, and two staves to the accompaniment. Treble voice parts are written in treble clef on pitches actually sounded. Tenor parts are written in treble clef an octave higher than they are to sound while Bass parts are written in bass clef on pitches actually sounded.

Full score is best for complex settings with many vocal parts as the division is difficult to show when there are more than two parts on a staff. It is also desirable in contrapuntal writing where each voice has its own line of text and where voice parts may cross.

The general pattern for full scoring of vocal parts, accompaniment, tempo and dynamic markings is illustrated in Ex. 236. Notice the position of all dynamic markings above each vocal staff and between the two staves of the piano. Note also the difference between the brackets encompassing choral and piano parts.

Ex. 236   "Holy, Holy, Holy"—J. Dykes, arr. R. Ringwald © Copyright MCMXLIV, Shawnee Press, Inc.

Condensed scoring

In dealing with harmonically simple materials, other forms of scoring are frequently adopted to conserve space, reduce page turns, and facilitate the accompanist's playing of the voice parts during rehearsal. Of these, the most common is condensed score in which treble voice parts are combined on a single treble staff and male voice parts on a single bass staff. Notes with stems up are assigned to Sopranos and Tenors, those with stems down to Altos and Basses. Piano accompaniment, when included, is assigned to two staves as in full scoring.

Condensed score is best suited to simple homophonic treatments with no more than four voice parts and a minimum of contrapuntal writing. It should be used only when the complete arrangement or extended sections thereof can be condensed without loss of clarity; frequent alternation between full and condensed score is confusing to the singers. Ex. 237 illustrates the condensed score.

Ex. 237   "Michael Finnigan" — arr. H. Ades

In Ex. 238 treble and male voices are combined on single stems whenever possible. Separate stems are used when voices move independently (Tenor part bar 2, beats 1 - 2) or when voices join in unison (Soprano and Altos parts, bar 2, beat 4). This type of scoring is commonly used in hymnals and community song books or wherever easy homophonic writing is found.

Ex. 238   "All Through the Night" — arr. H. Ades

Extended unison passages may be very simply scored as in Ex. 239.

Ex. 239   "Prayer of Thanksgiving"

Score markings

Alternations of volume and tempo

Crescendos — diminuendos and accelerandos — ritardandos of extended duration are indicated by their abbreviations followed by broken lines. Simultaneous increases or decreases in both tempo and dynamic level often include the term·*poco a poco* (little by little). Following markings which temporarily alter the tempo, the indication *a tempo* should mark the point of return to the normal tempo. In choral scoring these indications are shown above each vocal staff and between the staves of the accompaniment.

Signatures

Key signatures are used on each staff throughout the arrangement, but meter signatures are shown only at the beginning and at changes of meter. Ex. 240 gives the proper scoring of a simultaneous key and meter change.

Ex. 240   "Songs of Conquest" — H. Mc Donald
ⓒ Copyright MCMXXXVII, MCMXXXIX, Elkan-Vogel Co., copyright owners, Philadelphia, Pa.

Stemming

On staffs with only a single voice, notes written above the third line have stems turned down, notes written below the third line have stems turned up, and notes on the third line have stems turned up or down, depending on the contour of the melodic line. When several notes are joined by a beam, the stems turn up or down depending on whether the majority of the notes are above or below the third line.

When two voice parts are written on a single staff but sing different words, the text is shown for each voice above and below the staff for short passages only. If words are consistently different, voices should be assigned separate staves.

Flags and beams

It is traditional in vocal writing that flags are used on 8th and 16th notes when each carries a syllable of text, but notes are joined by beams and slurs when syllables are sustained for more than one tone. Recently and especially in rhythmically complex works, the traditional scoring for instruments is adopted and beams are used on voice parts. This greatly facilitates the reading of rhythms as the notes within one count can be quickly recognized. The following example illustrates both methods of scoring vocal parts. Note that the duration of syllables sustained for more than one tone is indicated by an extended line following the text.

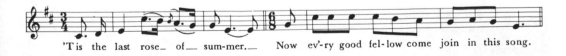

Breathing indications

Dotted slurs may be used to caution against taking a breath where it would break the textual or musical phrase. In long phrases, the instruction "stagger breathing" tells the singers to breathe at different places in the score to prevent breaking the flow of sound. The use of a breath comma above the staff marks desired breathing points.

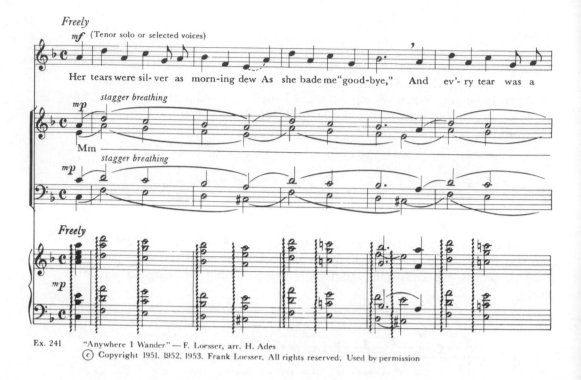

Ex. 241   "Anywhere I Wander" — F. Loesser, arr. H. Ades
© Copyright 1951, 1952, 1953. Frank Loesser, All rights reserved, Used by permission

Miscellaneous markings

Fermatas, tenutos, and all dynamic and temporary tempo change markings are indicated above all parts. Markings which apply to whole sections, indicating tempo, mood or style, are shown in two places only — over the voice parts and the accompaniment.

Ex. 242   "When Love Is Kind" — arr. H. Simeone,
© Copyright MCMLVI, Shawnee Press, Inc.

Ex. 243 illustrates scoring of a vocal glissando and also shows note heads for spoken or shouted words.

Ex. 243   "Three Village Scenes" — Bela Bartok
© Copyright 1927 by Universal Edition, Renewed 1954, Copyright & Renewal assigned to Boosey & Hawkes, Inc. for U.S.A. only. English translation by Martin Lindsay, Copyright 1954 by Boosey & Hawkes, Inc. Reprinted by permission.

A short line above a note indicates a slight stress or emphasis. (see Ex. 220.) The accent calls for a sharper and more sudden emphasis. (see Exs. 254, 304.) Staccato dots cut note values in half, replacing the second half with equivalent rests. (see Exs. 246, 254.)

Rehearsal letters are of great assistance to the conductor and should be included at intervals of approximately eight bars and at the beginning of sections or subsections in the music.

Careful attention to these details in scoring will result in an accurate presentation of the musical ideas, easier score reading by the conductor and singers, and therefore more effective performance.

SUMMARY

Proper scoring is essential to good performance; the major points to consider have been brought out in this chapter. Score markings are referred to because they vary to some extent between choral and instrumental writing. It should be emphasized that legible and correctly written manuscripts are part of the craft developed by a careful arranger.

Reference and Study Suggestions

Choosing one of the sketches you prepared for the last chapter, score the complete arrangement using full and condensed scoring where needed with all the proper markings. Give it the care you would if submitting it to a conductor or a publisher.

CHAPTER 18

CHORUS WITH INSTRUMENTAL GROUPS

AN infinite variety of combinations using voices with instrumental groups is possible and in many cases practical. Although the study of instrumental writing is beyond the scope of this book, the use of special instrumental groupings for choral accompaniments will be considered. The choral arranger should be familiar with the general types of instrumental accompaniments as discussed in this chapter.

The basic principles previously established in the chapter on accompaniments (see Chapter Two) apply equally to instrumental accompaniments. Particularly pertinent is the principle that the accompaniment must always enhance and never obscure the vocal presentation of the music and text. This principle must be stressed particularly in dealing with accompaniments where the sheer power of instruments can so easily overwhelm the choral sound.

In general it can be said that for most choral passages not rising above a mezzo forte, strings and—or woodwinds will provide an adequate body of sound for the accompaniment. In such passages, particularly in rhythmic numbers, occasional figurations may be assigned to the brass, either open or muted, depending upon the dynamic level. (See Ex. 247.)

Use of the brass as the primary basis for the accompaniment is ordinarily reserved for climactic forte or double forte sections where the power of these instruments is appropriate, but even here discretion is advisable. Scoring a choral unison will frequently be needed to insure that the chorus is not drowned out by a full brass accompaniment. (See Ex. 262.) When the chorus is singing in parts, a staccato style of accompaniment for the brass is often helpful in achieving clarity of choral sound and word projection. (See Ex. 254.) At other times, particularly for final cadences or other climactic points, the structure of the musical material and the demands of dramatic emphasis may require the use of sustained brass accompaniment with the fully harmonized chorus. The arranger should be aware of the dangers involved in such scoring, and then by skillful assignment of dynamics and tessituras make sure that the choral part can be heard.

Orchestral accompaniment

Orchestral accompaniment styles may be classified in much the same way as the accompaniments in Chapter Two. The following examples in condensed score indicate the general patterns of scoring for orchestra.

Accompaniments duplicating vocal parts

The simplest orchestral accompaniments are those in which the accompanying instruments exactly or approximately duplicate the vocal parts. In Ex. 244, the use of quiet strings with the voices adds warmth without disturbing the musical mood or obscuring clarity of the text. Such accompaniments should always be lightly scored, usually with only a single section of the orchestra.

Woodwinds blend best with girls' voices alone, and the tone quality of brass instruments combines well with male voices, though only a few brass instruments are needed to balance the male section. Strings occupy a middle ground and blend well with the full chorus as is illustrated in the following example. (See also Ex. 251A.)

Ex. 244   "Peer Gynt Suite" — E. Grieg, arr. H. Simeone

Ex. 245 illustrates orchestral doubling of choral parts to strengthen the various lines in a contrapuntal passage. Each line is scored for both string and woodwind instruments for neutral coloration. In this way the accompaniment effectively supports the choral parts without distracting from them as might a more colorful instrumentation.

Observe the text-painting in this strongly ascending passage.

Ex. 245   "Missa Solemnis" — L. van Beethoven

Rhythmic accompaniments

As with accompaniment styles for piano or organ, the melodic line is usually not included in accompaniments whose primary function is rhythmic; it would tend to obscure both the rhythmic movement and the clarity of melodic line in the vocal parts.

Our first example represents the typical "oom-pah" pattern commonly employed for bright, rhythmic music. Note the "hoe-down" countermelody for violins. If the orchestra does not include piano, the after-beats may be scored for 2nd violins and violas, though they are less effective in rhythmic backgrounds than the more percussive instruments (piano, drums, guitar, string bass pizz. etc.). Observe the absence of any sustained harmony in a passage where a brittle, purely rhythmic effect is desired.

Ex. 246   "The Song of America"—R. Ringwald,
      © Copyright MCMLI, Shawnee Press, Inc.

A second example of rhythmic accompaniment illustrates another basic pattern of scoring. In Example 247 the strings and woodwinds carry a simple countermelodic line while the muted brass are assigned figurations wherever the melodic line is stationary. Such use of brass avoids the danger of their obscuring the clarity of either melody or words. The brass may be either open or muted depending on the dynamic level of the particular passage.

Although the accompaniment of Ex. 248 is less obviously rhythmic in character, its primary function is to supply forward rhythmic impetus through the quiet reiteration of tones in a rhythmic pattern. A wide variety of rhythmic accompaniments based upon this principle is to be found in serious music.

Ex. 247   "Don't Fence Me In"—C. Porter
ⓒ Copyright MCMXLIV, Harms, Inc. Used by permission.

Ex. 248   "Requiem"—J. Brahms

Sustained accompaniments

Sustained accompaniments are often useful with choral unisons. In Ex. 249 strings and woodwinds adequately represent the harmonic structure while rhythmic impulse is supplied by rolled chords for harp and piano. In more robust passages, brass instruments might be preferable to strings and woodwinds.

Ex. 249   "Leprechaun's Lullaby"   G. Hurlburt, arr. H. Ades.
ⓒ Copyright MCMXLIX, Bregman, Vocco, & Conn, Inc.

Ex. 250 illustrates sustained accompaniment to a male voice unison in which the scoring for low brass and strings blends particularly well with the male voices. In a similar passage for treble voices, woodwinds as accompanying instruments would blend better.

Ex. 250   "Elijah" — F. Mendelssohn

Melodic accompaniments

Some accompaniments suggest neither rhythmic nor sustained treatment, but require considerable harmonic fullness and some strengthening of the melodic line. Such accompaniments should be scored to represent fairly completely the structure of the musical material. This is illustrated by the simple, but effective scoring for strings and bassoon only in Ex. 251A.

The imaginative orchestral accompaniment to the same theme as it appears later in the work is shown in Ⓑ The melodic line is now assigned to the flute in the upper octave while the moving violin figuration effectively enhances the meaning of the text.

Ex. 251   "The Seasons"— F. Haydn

Ex. 252 uses a rhythmic diminution of the melodic line in the accompaniment. This procedure is frequently useful in melodies with reiterated notes which require a fairly full accompaniment. The presence in the accompaniment of the outlines of the melodic and harmonic structure gives the required fullness without obstructing word clarity.

The opposite treatment may be used to achieve a strongly pulsating rhythmic surge in the accompaniment. In Ex. 253 the insistent brass figuration represents a rhythmic augmentation of the melodic line. Such full scoring is appropriate only for broad maestoso passages. It is usually reserved for the concluding section of an arrangement where it lends to the final entrance of the principal theme a dramatic sense of breadth and power.

Ex. 252   "Song of the Trolley" — M. Park

Ex. 253   "The Holy City" — A. Adams, arr. R. Ringwald,   © Copyright MCMXLVIII, Shawnee Press, Inc.

Punctuation as accompaniment

This type of scoring is particularly useful for songs with considerable melodic movement. Such accompaniments consist of orchestral chords which merely outline the harmonic and rhythmic structure and do not obscure the text. This technique is useful at any dynamic level. In quiet passages strings and woodwinds should be used while in more powerful passages, such as Ex. 254, the brass may be used effectively without obscuring the words.

Ex. 254   "The Song of America"—*op. cit.*

Ex. 255   "Elijah"—F. Mendelssohn, arr. H. Ades

Arpeggiated accompaniments

Ex. 255 illustrates the simplest treatment of an arpeggiated accompaniment in which the figuration is assigned to the harp, while bassoons, horns and strings support the melodic line and add sustaining quality.

Ex. 256 illustrates a more complex form of arpeggiated accompaniment. In this fortissimo passage, brass horns and bassoons support the chorus, while the arpeggios for divided strings provide dramatic sweeps downward and upward. Repeated quarter notes in cellos and basses provide rhythmic movement.

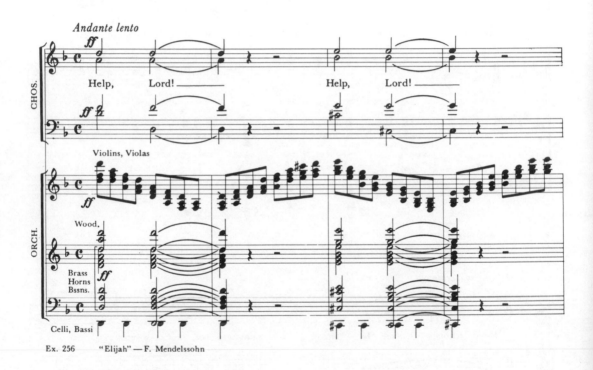

Ex. 256   "Elijah" — F. Mendelssohn

Figuration as accompaniment

Of the wide variety of figurated accompaniments which may be devised, two illustrations indicate the possibilities of this technique.

In Ex. 257, strings and low woodwinds support the general pattern of the vocal parts, while the eighth-note figuration for high woodwinds adds rhythmic drive and brightness of color.

In Ex. 258 woodwinds and low strings support the choral parts while violins carry an expressive figuration effectively enhancing the musical theme and text.

Ex. 257   "Liebeslieder Waltzes" — J. Brahms

Ex. 258   "Requiem Mass" — W. Mozart

Contrapuntal accompaniments

These accompaniments involve the use of countermelodic lines so strongly individual that they give the writing a predominantly contrapuntal character. Ex. 259 illustrates the effectiveness of such scoring utilizing a unison line for brass, strings and woodwinds as countermelody. Such striking effects should usually be reserved for the later stages of an arrangement after the melody and words have been established and there is need to build interest.

Ex. 259   "The Old Black Magic"—H. Arlen, arr. R. Ringwald,
© Copyright 1942, Famous Music Corporation

Special effects in accompaniment

The range of possibilities in this area defies exhaustive analysis and three examples of the scoring of special effects must suffice. Ex. 260 is an animated accompaniment suggestive of sleigh bells, and appropriate to the musical and textual material of the composition.

Ex. 260   "Grandma's Thanksgiving"—H. Simeone
© Copyright MCMXLVII, Shawnee Press, Inc

Ex. 261 illustrates the use of an agitated figuration for strings to establish mood for the textual idea to follow. It is interesting to see how often the great composers make use of such text-painting.

Ex. 261   "Elijah" — F. Mendelssohn

In Ex. 262 the brass section is used for a powerful dramatic effect appropriate to the text. Observe the choral unison to insure that the vocal line will not be overpowered by the brass figuration.

Ex. 262   "The Song of Easter" — R. Ringwald,
        ⓒ Copyright MCMXLIX, Shawnee Press, Inc.

Accompaniment in climactic passages

Special mention should be made of some of the problems of scoring climactic passages in which the use of full orchestral accompaniment may tend to over-power the chorus. Such passages often occur at the final cadences of arrangements or compositions where the demands of dramatic emphasis require the use of the full orchestra. (See Ex. 263.) It is important, however, to maintain textual clarity even in climactic passages and the following examples indicate possible solutions.

Ex. 263   "Give Me a Place in the Sun" — F. Waring
        ⓒ Copyright MCMXLVIII, Shawnee Press, Inc.

The simplest approach to this problem uses the unaccompanied chorus in the concluding bars of an arrangement, reserving orchestral power for an instrumental "tag" following the final choral cadence. A few measures of unaccompanied voices in this position can often prove highly effective and also provide a dramatic color contrast for the final entrance of the orchestra.

Where word clarity is essential but unaccompanied choral scoring seems inadvisable, a sustained or contrapuntal accompaniment fairly full and scored in a rather low register, will supply a solid background and provide ample sonority. This allows the chorus to soar above the accompaniment and preserves word clarity. Observe in Ex. 264 the dramatic impact of the entrance of the trumpets on an independent line just before the final choral cadence.

Ex. 264   "The Song of America"—*op. cit.*

Chorus as orchestral color

This is an area of arranging which has been inadequately exploited and one which offers to the enterprising arranger many interesting possibilities for experimentation. In this style the orchestra and chorus are combined into a single integral unit with voices used as a section of the orchestra. Considerable broadening of the orchestral palette is made possible through this utilization of choral sounds as orchestral color. Within the vocal section a variety of colors can be achieved using instrumental sounds or groups of neutral vowels; the interjection of occasional short phrases of words provides dramatic emphasis. The chorus may be assigned melodic lines, countermelodies, figurations, accompaniment patterns or any other musical device accessible to voices. The following example gives some indication of the possibilities of writing for the chorus as a section within the orchestra.

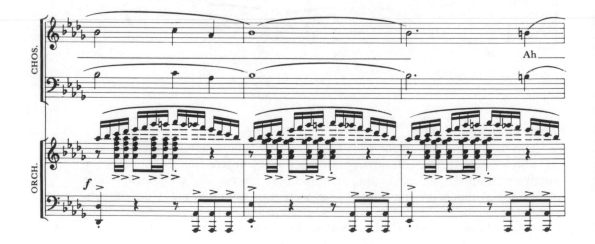

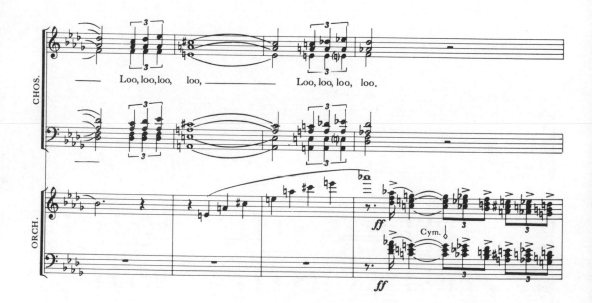

Ex. 265   "Jalousie" — J. Gade, arr. H. Simeone
Copyright MCMXXVI, T.B. Harms, Inc.
© MCMXXV by Gade & Wamys Musikforlag
© MCMXXVI by Edition Charles Brull, Paris, © MCMXXXI by Harms, Inc.
Used by permission.

Band and chorus

The principles governing the writing of arrangements for band and chorus are basically similar to those discussed for orchestra and chorus with such distinctions as are necessitated by differences in instrumentation. Passages which would be assigned to strings in the orchestra will be scored for E flat clarinets, B flat clarinets, bass clarinets and bassoon in the band. Ochestral woodwind passages will be assigned in the band to piccolos, flutes, oboes and bassoons. The precaution regarding the use of brass in orchetral accompaniments applies with even greater force to scoring for band because of the greater predominance of brass instruments.

The following example illustrates the scoring of a tutti passage for chorus and band.

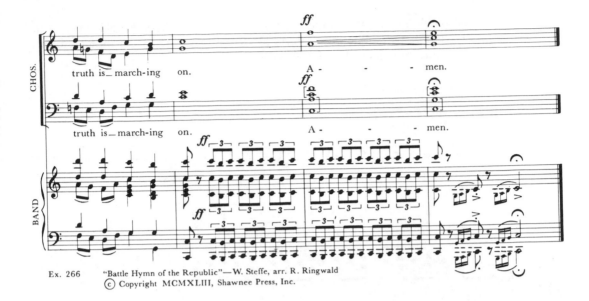

Ex. 266   "Battle Hymn of the Republic"—W. Steffe, arr. R. Ringwald
           © Copyright MCMXLIII, Shawnee Press, Inc.

Chorus with small instrumental groups

There are great possibilities for color and dramatic interest through the use of single instruments or small groups of instruments as accompaniment for choral arrangements. Such instrumental coloring will often enhance the expressive quality of the arrangement.

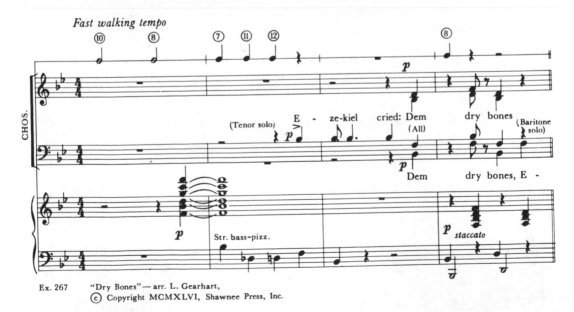

Ex. 267   "Dry Bones"—arr. L. Gearhart,
           © Copyright MCMXLVI, Shawnee Press, Inc.

Ex. 267 illustrates an effective though unusual use of percussion instruments. The following are used at various times within the arrangement: (1) Temple blocks, (2) ratchet, (3) muffled cowbell, (4) xylophone, (5) chime, (6) bell,

(7) wood block, (8) length of pipe, (9) triangle, (10) small wood block, (11) casta-net, (12) xylophone (single note). Parts for these instruments are indicated on a percussion line on which their numbers appear.

Violin as accompaniment color

Ex. 268   "Mr. Frog" — arr. L. Gearheart.
© Copyright MCMXLVIII, Shawnee Press, Inc.

See also Ex. 135 where a similar treatment uses guitar and string bass — the two best supplementary accompanying instruments for supporting rhythmic arrangements.

Sleigh bells and a string bass

Ex. 269   "Jingle Bells" — arr. H. Simeone, *op cit.*

Woodblock as accompaniment color

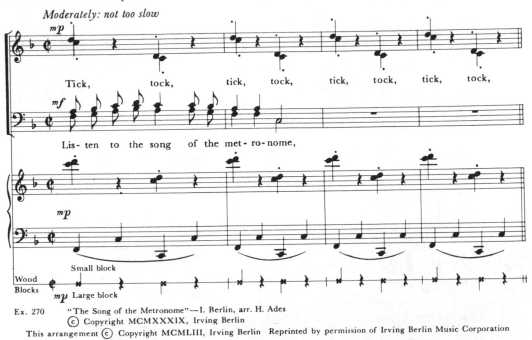

Ex. 270   "The Song of the Metronome"—I. Berlin, arr. H. Ades
ⓒ Copyright MCMXXXIX, Irving Berlin
This arrangement ⓒ Copyright MCMLIII, Irving Berlin Reprinted by permission of Irving Berlin Music Corporation

A complete arrangement or section for solo instrument with choral accompaniment is often effective in achieving contrast and variety in a choral program. A choral accompaniment for violin solo is illustrated in Ex. 271.

"Cavatina"—J. Raff, arr. F. Buckner,
Ex. 271   ⓒ Copyright MCML, Shawnee Press, Inc.

Three trumpets and percussion

Ex. 272   "God of Our Fathers" — W. Warren, arr. L. Gearhart.
ⓒ Copyright MCMXLIX, Shawnee Press, Inc.

SUMMARY

Classification of orchestral accompaniments and illustrating the use of some special instrumental combinations have been the major considerations in Chapter Eighteen. It must be made clear that the choral arranger does not necessarily need a thorough instrumental background to achieve effective results from various combinations. However, without knowledge of instrumental ranges, timbre, and suitable technical information, he may find himself in difficulty if his first efforts are too ambitious. Experience with instrumentalists and the study of numerous examples will prepare the way for an arranger to complete some fascinating choral-instrumental experiments.

Reference and Study Suggestions

1. Select simple folk tunes as the basis for short arrangements with the following accompaniments:
   a) brass only
   b) woodwinds only
   c) strings only

2. Devise an imaginative accompaniment with a small but unusual instrumental grouping in an arrangement of a patriotic song. You may wish to use the arrangement from the Study Suggestions of Chapter Six.

3. Sketch a plan for the arrangement of a strong melodic idea (patriotic, chorale, familiar standard song) using mixed voices and either band or orchestra accompaniment.

BIBLIOGRAPHY

Davison, Archibald T. *The Technique of Choral Composition* – Cambridge: Harvard University Press, 1945

Delamont, Gordon. *Modern Arranging Techniques* – Delevan, N. Y.: Kendor Music, 1965

Forsyth, Cecil. *Orchestration* – New York: The Macmillan Co., 1942

Goetschius, Percy. *The Theory and Practice of Tone-relations* – New York: G. Schirmer, Inc., 1927

Kauder, Hugo. *Counterpoint* –New York: The Macmillan Co., 1960

Kitson, Charles H. *Six Lectures on Accompanied Choral Writing* – London: Oxford University Press, 1930

Kitson, Charles H. *The Art of Counterpoint* – London: Oxford University Press, 1924

Lang, Philip J. *Scoring for the Band* – New York: Mills Music, Inc., 1950

McKenzie, Duncan. *Training the Boy's Changing Voice* – New Brunswick: Rutgers University Press, 1956

Miller, Horace A. *New Harmonic Devices* – Boston: Oliver Ditson Co., 1930

Miller, Horace A. *Modal Trends in Modern Music* – Cornell Music Publishing Co., 1941

Read, Gardner. *Music Notation* – Boston: Allyn and Bacon, Inc., 1964

Piston, Walter. *Harmony* – New York: W. W. Norton, 1944

Piston, Walter. *Counterpoint* – New York: W. W. Norton, 1947

Prout, Ebenezer. *Counterpoint* – London: Augener and Co., 1900

Prout, Ebenezer. *Double Counterpoint and Canon* – London: Augener and Co., 1891

Rimsky-Korsakoff, Nicolas. *Principles of Orchestration* – New York: E. F. Kalmus Orchestra Scores, Inc., 1914

Serly, Tibor. *A Second Look at Harmony* – New York: Forrell and Thomas, 1964

Sessions, Roger. *Harmonic Practice* – New York: Harcourt, Brace and World 1951

Wilson, Harry R. *Choral Arranging* – New York: Robbins Music Corp., 1949

Young, Percy M. *The Choral Tradition* – London: Hutchinson & Co., 1962

APPENDIX
SUPPLEMENTARY EXAMPLES

Traditional Four-Part Writing

Bach, Johann Sebastian, *Mass In B Minor* — H. W. Gray Co., Inc.
  No. 3. Kyrie eleison — Letter B. Bars 1-11.

Bartok, Bela, *Four Slovak Folk Songs* — Boosey & Hawkes, Ltd.
  No. 1. Bars 40-55.

Brahms, Johannes, *Requiem* — G. Schirmer, Inc.
  No. 1. Bars 15-27.

Delius, Frederic, *Sea Drift* — Boosey & Hawkes, Ltd.
  No. 3 Bars 4-12.

Foss, Lukas, *The Prairie* — G. Schirmer, Inc.
  Part II. Dust of men — Bars 115-131.

Handel, George Frederick, *The Messiah* — G. Schirmer, Inc.
  No. 44. Hallelujah — Bars 3-10.

Haydn, Josef, *The Creation* — G. Schirmer, Inc.
  No. 14. The Heavens are telling — Bar 1 ff.

Hindemith, Paul, *Apparebit Repentina Dies* — Schott & Co. Ltd.
  Part IV. Bars 2-14.

Holst, Gustav, *1st Choral Symphony* — London Novello & Co., Ltd.
  No. II. Ode on a Grecian urn — No. 28 Bar 1 ff.

Mendelssohn, Felix, *Elijah* — G. Schirmer, Inc.
  No. 15. Cast thy burden upon the Lord — Bar 1 ff.

Mozart, Wolfgang Amadeus, *Requiem Mass* — H. W. Gray Co., Inc.
  No. 2. Dies irae — Bar 1 ff.

Poulenc, Francis, *Secheresses* — Durand & Co.
  No. 1. Les sauterelles — Bars 22-29, 107-113.

Thompson, Randall, *Five Odes Of Horace* — E. C. Schirmer Music Co.
  Vitas hinnuleo — Bar 7 ff., 36 ff.

Verdi, Giuseppe, *Requiem* — G. Schirmer, Inc.
  No 2. Day of anger — Bars 31-39.

Walton, William, *Belshazzar's Feast* — Oxford University Press.
  No. 21 Bars 1-9.

Harmonization in Parallel Motion

Hindemith, Paul, *Apparebit Repentina Dies* — Schott & Co., Ltd.
  Part I. Bars 117-126.

Honegger, Arthur, *King David* — E. C. Schirmer Music Co.
  No. 4. Song of Victory — Bars 2-3, 5-6, 8.

Milhaud, Darius, *Miracles Of Faith* — G. Schirmer, Inc.
Introduction — Bars 29-30.

Poulenc, Francis, *Secheresses* — Durand & Co.
Part III. Le faux avenir — Bars 215-219, 235-236.

Walton, William, *Belshazzar's Feast* — Oxford University Press.
No. 15. Bars 1-6.

CHAPTER THREE   ACCOMPANIMENTS

Accompaniments Duplicating Vocal Parts

Beethoven, Ludwig von, *Missa Solemnis In D* — G. Schirmer, Inc.
Credo — Letter Bb. Bar 2 ff.

Dello Joio, Norman, *Song Of The Open Road* — Carl Fischer, Inc.
Bar 15 ff.

Handel, George Frederick, *The Messiah* — G. Schirmer, Inc.
No. 25. And with His stripes — Bar 1 ff.

Mozart, Wolfgang Amadeus, *Requiem Mass* — H. W. Gray Co., Inc.
No. 10. Sanctus — Bar 11 ff.

Verdi, Giuseppe, *Requiem* — G. Schirmer, Inc.
Requiem and kyrie — Letter B Bar 1 ff.

Walton, William, *Belshazzar's Feast* — Oxford University Press.
Bar 3 ff.

Rhythmic Accompaniments

Borodin, Alexander, *Prince Igor* — Boosey & Hawkes, Ltd.
Choral Dance No. 17 — Letter W. Bar 1 ff.

Brahms, Johannes, *Requiem* — G. Schirmer, Inc.
No. III. Letter B Bars 16-33.

Haydn, Josef, *The Creation* — G. Schirmer, Inc.
No. 2. In the beginning — Bar 17 ff.
No. 29. (continued) — Of stars the fairest — Last 17 bars.

Honegger, Arthur, *King David* — E. C. Schirmer Music Co.
No. 11. Psalm — No. 2 Bar 1 ff.
No. 19. Psalm of penitence — Bar 1 ff.
No. 22. The song of Ephraim — Bar 1 ff.

Mendelssohn, Felix, *Elijah* — G. Schirmer, Inc.
No. 1. Help, Lord — Bar 36 ff.
No. 12. Call Him louder — Bar 13 ff.
No. 34. Behold, God the Lord — Bar 10 ff.
No. 38. Then did Elijah — Bar 1 ff.

Prokofieff, Serge, *Alexander Nevsky* — Leeds Music Corp.
No. 2. Song about Alexander Nevsky — Bar 8 ff.
No. 5. The battle on ice — No. ⬚38 Bar 1 ff.

Vaughan Williams, Ralph, *A Sea Symphony* — Stainer and Bell, Ltd.
No. 1. A song for all seas, all ships — Letter ⬚A Bar 5 ff.

Verdi, Giuseppe, *Requiem* — G. Schirmer, Inc.
Day of Anger — Letter ⬚B Bar 1 ff.

Walton, William, *Belshazzar's Feast* — Oxford University Press.
No. ⬚10 Bar 1 ff, No. ⬚70 Bar 2 ff, No. ⬚76 Bar 1 ff.

Melodic Accompaniments

Borodin, Alexander, *Prince Igor* — Boosey & Hawkes, Ltd.
Choral Dance No. 17 — Letter ⬚A Bar 1 ff, Letter ⬚U Bar 1 ff.

Brahms, Johannes, *Requiem* — G. Schirmer, Inc.
No. IV. Bars 5-13.
No. VI. Bar 3 ff.

Handel, George Frederick, *The Messiah* — G. Schirmer, Inc.
No. 26. All we like sheep — Bar 1 ff.

Haydn, Josef, *The Creation* — G. Schirmer, Inc.
No. 5. The marv'lous work — Bar 16 ff.
No. 14. The Heavens are telling — Bar 1 ff.

Haydn, Josef, *The Seasons* — G. Schirmer, Inc.
No. 3. Come, gentle Spring — Bar 5 ff.

Honegger, Arthur, *King David* — E. C. Schirmer Music Co.
No. 27. The death of David — Letter ⬚B Bar 1 ff.

Mendelssohn, Felix, *Elijah* — G. Schirmer, Inc.
No. 11. Baal, we cry to thee — Bar 1 ff.
No. 22. Be not afraid — Bar 1 ff.

Prokofieff, Serge, *Alexander Nevsky* — Leeds Music Corp.
No. 4. Arise, ye Russian people — No. ⬚31 Bars 1-9.
No. 7. Alexander's entry in Pskov — No. ⬚7 Bar 1 ff.

Vaughan Williams, Ralph, *A Sea Symphony* — Stainer and Bell, Ltd.
No. III. The waves — Letter ⬚K Bar 1 ff.

Verdi, Giuseppe, *Requiem* — G. Schirmer, Inc.
Day of anger — Letter ⬚A Bar 1 ff.

Sustained Accompaniments

Brahms, Johannes, *Requiem* — G. Schirmer, Inc.
No. III. Letter ⬚B Bars 1-6, 9-15, Letter ⬚F Bars 1-6, 21-26.

Honegger, Arthur, *King David* — E. C. Schirmer Music Co.
No. 20. Psalm — No. 1 Bars 1-4.

Mendelssohn, Felix, *Elijah* — G.Schirmer, Inc.
No. 1. Help, Lord — Last 11 bars.
No. 35. Holy is God the Lord — Bars 16-20.
No. 36. Go, return upon thy way — Bars 1-9.
No. 41. But the Lord from the North — Bars 2-7.

Broken Accompaniments

Beethoven, Ludwig von, *Missa Solemnis* In D — G. Schirmer, Inc.
Gloria — Letter OO Bar 1 ff.

Brahms, Johannes, *Requiem* — G. Schirmer, Inc.
No. III. Letter C Bar 2 ff.

Handel, George Frederick, *The Messiah* — G. Schirmer, Inc.
No. 39. Their sound is gone out into all lands — Bars 1-4.

Holst, Gustav, *King Estmere* — Charles Avison, Ltd.
No. 1 Bars 1-8.

Honegger, Arthur, *King David* — E. C. Schirmer Music Co.
No. 25. Psalm — Bar 13 ff.

Mendelssohn, Felix, *Elijah* — G. Schirmer, Inc.
No. 13. Call him louder! — Last 12 bars.
No. 23. The Lord hath exalted thee — Last 4 bars.

Arpeggiated Accompaniments

Bartok, Bela, *Four Slovak Folk Songs* — Boosey & Hawkes, Ltd.
No. I. Bar 41 ff.

Haydn, Josef, *The Seasons* — G. Schirmer, Inc.
No. 7. Be propitious, bounteous Heaven — Letter F Bar 4 ff.

Mendelssohn, Felix, *Elijah* — G. Schirmer, Inc.
No. 1. Help, Lord — Bars 1-9.
No. 19-A. Thou hast overthrown Thine enemies — Bar 48 ff.
No. 29. He, watching over Israel — Bar 1 ff.

Vaughan Williams, Ralph, *A Sea Symphony* — Stainer and Bell, Ltd.
No. I. A song for all seas, all ships — Bar 5 ff.
No. IV. The explorers — Letter W Bar 14 ff.

Verdi, Giuseppe, *Requiem* — G. Schirmer, Inc.
Holy — Letter A Bar 7 ff.

Figuration as Accompaniment

Bach, Johann Sebastian, *Mass In B Minor* — H. W. Gray Co., Inc.
No. 15. Et incarnatus est — Bar 1 ff.

Bartok, Bela, *Four Slovak Folk Songs* – Boosey & Hawkes, Ltd.
No. 11. Bars 1-6.

Beethoven, Ludwig von, *Missa Solemnis In D* – G. Schirmer, Inc.
Agnus Dei — Letter $\boxed{W}$ Bars 4-10, Letter $\boxed{Y}$ Bars 1-11.

Brahms, Johannes, *Requiem* – G. Schirmer, Inc.
No. VI. Letter $\boxed{L}$ Bars 2-12.

Haydn, Josef, *The Creation* – G. Schirmer, Inc.
No. 29. Dy Thee with bliss — Bar 24 ff.

Holst, Gustav, *1st Choral Symphony* – London Novello & Co., Ltd.
No. I. Song and bacchanal — No. 16. Bar 1 ff.

Honegger, Arthur, *King David* – E. C. Schirmer Music Co.
No. 15. Song of the daughters of Israel — Bar 8 ff.

Mendelssohn, Felix, *Elijah* – G. Schirmer, Inc.
No. 38. Then did Elijah — Bar 34 ff.
No. 41.. But the Lord from the North — Bar 13 ff.

Vaughan Williams, Ralph, *A Sea Symphony* – Stainer and Bell, Ltd.
No. I. A song for all seas — Letter $\boxed{Bb}$ Bar 11 ff, Letter $\boxed{Cc}$ Bar 7 ff.
No. IV. The explorers — Letter $\boxed{R}$ Bar 4 ff.

Contrapuntal Accompaniments

Bach, Johann Sebastian, *Mass In B Minor* – H. W. Gray Co., Inc.
No. 1. Kyrie eleison — Bar 30 ff.

Beethoven, Ludwig von, *Missa Solemnis In D* — G. Schirmer, Inc.
Agnus Dei — Letter $\boxed{Bb}$ Bar 1 ff, Letter $\boxed{I}$ Bar 1 ff, Letter $\boxed{L}$ Bar 1 ff.

Borodin, Alexander, *Prince Igor* — Boosey & Hawkes, Ltd.
Choral Dance No. 17 — Letter $\boxed{P}$ Bar 1 ff.

Handel, George Frederick, *The Messiah* – G. Schirmer, Inc.
No. 7. He shall purify — Bar 1 ff.
No. 17. Glory to God — Bars 1-4.

Haydn, Josef, *The Creation* – G. Schirmer, Inc.
No. 14. The Heavens are telling — Bar 38 ff.

Holst, Gustav, *1st Choral Symphony* – London Novello & Co., Ltd.
Prelude — Bar 5 ff.
No. I. Song and bacchanal — No. 18 Bar 3 ff.

Honegger, Arthur, *King David* — E. C. Schirmer Music Co.
No. 3. Psalm — Bars 2-11.

Milhaud, Darius, *Miracles of Faith* — G. Schirmer, Inc.
Introduction — Bars 11-15.
Part 3. Daniel and Darius — Bar 170 ff.

Mozart, Wolfgang Amadeus, *Requiem Mass* — H. W. Gray Co., Inc.
No. 4. Rex Tremendae — Bar 1 ff.

Prokofieff, Serge, *Alexander Nevsky* — Leeds Music Co.
No. 5. The Battle on Ice — No. 48 Bar 2 ff.

Vaughan Williams, Ralph, *A Sea Symphony* — Stainer and Bell, Ltd.
No. III. The Waves — Letter Z Bars 1-12
No. IV. The Explorers — Letter H Bars 4-14.

Special Effects In Accompaniment

Brahms, Johannes, *Requiem* — G. Schirmer, Inc.
No. II. Letter D Bars 22-29.

Haydn, Josef, *The Creation* — G. Schirmer, Inc.
No. 7. Rolling in Foaming Billows — Bar 13 ff.

Haydn, Josef, *The Seasons* — G. Schirmer, Inc.
No. 21. Hark, the deep tremendous voice — Bars 3-8.
No. 40. Let the wheel roll gaily — Bar 5 ff.

Holst, Gustav, *1st Choral Symphony* — London Novello & Co.
No. IV. Finale — No. 60 Bars 2-5.

Mendelssohn, Felix, *Elijah* — G. Schirmer, Inc.
No. 16. O Thou, who mak'st thine angels spirits — Bar 6 ff.
No. 20. Thanks be to God! Bar 20 ff.

Verdi, Giuseppi, *Requiem* — G. Schirmer, Inc.
Day of anger — Letter C Bars 29-34.
Light eternal — Bar 1 ff.

Organ Accompaniments

Britten, Benjamin, *Festival Te Deum* — Boosey & Hawkes, Inc.

Elgar, Sir Edward, *Great Is the Lord* — London Novello and Co.

Ellingford, Arthur, *The Art of Transcribing for the Organ* — H. W. Gray Co., Inc.

Franck, Cesar, *Psalme CL* — Nevelle, Fortemps et Cie.

Hanson, Howard, *How Excellent Thy Name* — Carl Fischer, Inc.

Sowerby, Leo, *The Pilgrim Pavement* — H. W. Gray Co., Inc.

Sowerby, Leo *My Heart is Fixed* — H. W. Gray Co., Inc.

Vaughan Williams, Ralph, *The Pilgrim Pavement* — Oxford University Press.

Vaughan Williams, Ralph, *The Voice Out of the Whirlwind* — Oxford University Press.

Yon, Pietro, *Our Paschal Joy* — J. Fischer & Bro.

Four-Hand Accompaniments

Brahms, Johannes, *Liebeslieder Waltzes* — Boosey & Hawkes, Inc.

Traditional Three-Part Writing

Bartok. Bela. *Four Slovak Folk Songs* — Boosey and Hawkes, Ltd.
    No. III. Bars 21-28.

Foss, Lukas, *The Prairie* — G. Schirmer, Inc.
    Part VI. Cool Prayers — Bars 14-22.

Harris, Roy, *Blow the Man Down* — Carl Fischer, Inc.
    Bars 214-218, 245-249.

Haydn, Josef, *The Seasons* — G. Schirmer, Inc.
    No. 7. Be Propitious, Bounteous Heaven — Letter B Bars 18-22.
    No. 9. Spring, Her Lovely Charms Unfolding — Letter D Bars 2-8.
    No. 31. Hark! How the mountains resound — Letter B Bars 2-9, 15-18.

Hindemith, Paul, *Apparebit Repentina Dies* — Schott and Co., Ltd.
    Part II. Bars 42-52, 94-109.
    Part III. Bars 106-115.

Holst, Gustav, *1st Choral Symphony* — London Novello & Co., Ltd.
    Prelude — No. 4 Bars 3-6.
    No. I. Song and Bacchanal — No. 12 Bars 7-11.
    No. III. Scherzo — No. 39 Bars 14-20.

Honegger, Arthur, *King David* — E. C. Schirmer Music Co.
    No. 16. The Dance Before the Ark. No. 7 Bars 1-4.

Malipiero, Gian Francesco, *La Terra* — Edizioni Suvini Zerboni.
    Bars 244-247.

McDonald, Harl, *Songs of Conquest* — Elkan-Vogel Co., Inc.
    No. II. A Complaint against the bitterness — Bar 6 ff.
    No. IV. The exaltation of man — Bars 3-7, 51-63.

Respighi, Ottorino, *La Primavera* — Universal-Edition.
    No.7 Bars 1-13. No. 38 Bars 1-5, 13-16.
    No. 63 Bars 6-9.

Parallel Three-Part Writing

Copland, Aaron, *Lark* — E. C. Schirmer Music Co.
    Last 7 Bars.

Holst, Gustav, *1st Choral Symphony* — London Novello & Co., Ltd.
    No. II. Ode on a Grecian urn — No. 25 Bars 7-10. No. 26 Bars 1-7.

Malipiero, Gian Francesco, *Vergilii Aeneis* — Edizioni Suvini Zerboni.
    Bars 1018-1022.

Prokofieff, Serge, *Alexander Nevsky* —Leeds Music Co.
    No. 5. The Battle on Ice — No. 43 Bars 1-5. No. 44 Bars 1-2.

Respighi, Ottorino, *La Primavera* — Universal -Edition.
    No. 8 Bars 11-18.

Vaughan Williams, Ralph, *A Sea Symphony* — Stainer and Bell, Ltd.
No. III. The waves — Bars 3-7, 11-14.

CHAPTER FIVE   TWO-PART WRITING

Traditional Two-Part Writing

Handel, George Frederick, *The Messiah* — G. Schirmer, Inc.
No. 33. Lift Up Your Heads — Letter A Bars 1-5.

Harris, Roy, *Blow the Man Down* — Carl Fischer, Inc.
Bars 126-128, 317-321.

Haydn, Josef, *The Seasons* — G. Schirmer, Inc.
No. 9. Spring, Her Lovely Charms Unfolding — Letter C Bars 6-17.
No. 31. Hark! How the mountains resound — Bars 15-20. Letter A
Bars 2-17.
No. 33 Joyful the liquor flows — Letter A Bars 2-11. Letter C Bars 2-6.
Letter D Bars 6-13. Letter E Bars 2-12, 17 ff.

Hindemith, Paul, *Apparebit Repentina Dies* — Schott & Co., Ltd.
Part III. Bars 100-105.

Honegger, Arthur, *King David* — E. C. Schirmer Music Co.
No. 8. Song of the Prophets — Bars 1-5.
No. 11. Psalm — Bars 2-6, 10-14.
No. 16 The Dance Before the Ark — No. 5 Bars 1-8.

McDonald, Harl, *Songs of Conquest* — Elkan-Vogel Co., Inc.
No. 1. The Breadth and Extent of Man's Empire — Bars 39-44.

Mozart, Wolfgang Amadeus, *Requiem Mass* — H. W. Gray Co., Inc.
No. 6 Confutatis Maledictis — Bars 7-10, 17-25.

Prokofieff, Serge, *Alexander Nevsky* — Leeds Music Corp.
No. 4. Arise, Ye Russian People — No. 25 Bars 5-17, No. 29 Bars 1-8.
No. 7. Alexander's Entry in Pskov — No. 82 Bars 1-6.

Respighi, Ottorino, *La Primavera* — Universal-Edition.
No. 8 Bars 7-10, No. 34 Bars 6-17, No. 35 Bar 2 ff.

Thompson, Randall, *Five Odes of Horace* — E. C. Schirmer Music Co.
Vitas Hinnuleo — Bars 20-27.

Walton, William, *Belshazzar's Feast* — Oxford University Press.
No. 20 Bars 1-4, No. 58 Bars 5-10, No. 59 Bars 2-6, No. 76 Bars 5-11.

Parallel Two-Part Writing

Beethoven, Ludwig von, *Missa Solemnis in D* — G. Schirmer, Inc.
Gloria — Letter U Bars 17-20, 25-26.

Borodin, Alexander, *Prince Igor - Choral Dance No. 17* — Boosey and Hawkes, Ltd. — Letter V Bars 1-8.

Brahms, Johannes, *Requiem* — G. Schirmer, Inc.
No. II. Letter A Bars 11-12, Letter B Bars 23-25.

Holst, Gustav, *1st Choral Symphony* — London Novello & Co., Ltd.
No. IV. Finale — No. 62 Bars 5-8.

Mendelssohn, Felix, *Elijah* — G. Schirmer, Inc.
No. 11. Baal, we cry to thee — Last 9 Bars.
No. 13. Baal! Baal! — Bars 1-4.

Prokofieff, Serge, *Alexander Nevsky* — Leeds Music Co.
No. 2. Song about Alexander Nevsky — Bars 8-12.

Respighi, Ottorino, *La Primavera* — Universal-Edition.
No. 63 Bars 1-5.

Thompson, Randall, *Five Odes of Horace* — E. C. Schirmer Music Co.
O fons bandusiae — Bars 1-5.

Vaughan Williams, Ralph, *A Sea Symphony* — Stainer and Bell, Ltd.
No. I. A Song for all seas — Letter L Bars 1-4.
No. III. The waves — Letter D Bars 8-12.

Traditional Two-Part Writing in Octaves

Prokofieff, Serge, *Alexander Nevsky* — Leeds Music Co.
No. 4. Arise, Ye Russian People — No. 24 Bars 5-13.
No. 7. Alexander's Entry in Pskov — No. 80 Bars 1-5, No. 89 Bars 8-12.

Sowerby, Leo, *Song for America* — The H. W. Gray Co., Inc.
Letter M Bars 1-7.

Walton, William, *In Honour of the City of London* — Oxford University Press.
No. 18 Bars 3-13.

Walton, William, *Belshazzar's Feast* — Oxford University Press
No. 17 Bars 1-5, No. 76 Bars 4-11.

Parallel Two-Part Writing in Octaves

Brahms, Johannes, *Requiem* — G. Schirmer, Inc.
No. II. Letter D Bars 29-33.
No. VI. Letter A Bars 13-16.

Dello Joio, Norman, *A Jubilant Song* — G. Schirmer, Inc.
Bars 27-36.

Milhaud, Darius, *Barba Garibo* — Heugel et Cie.
Le Romarin Fleuri — Bars 116-123.

220

Strong Melodic Line

Beethoven, Ludwig von, *Chorale Finale To Ninth Symphony* — G. Schirmer, Inc.
    Andante maestoso — Bars 2-9.

Borodin, Alexander, *Prince Igor* — Boosey & Hawkes, Ltd.
    Choral dance No. 17 — Letter D Bars 16-19, Letter K Bars 1-16,
    Letter Y Bars 1-12.

Brahms, Johannes, *Schicksalslied* — H. W. Gray Co., Inc.
    Allegro — Bars 8-29.

Handel, George Frederick, *The Messiah* — G. Schirmer, Inc.
    No. 44. Hallelujah — Bars 12-14, 17-19.

Haydn, Josef, *The Creation* — G. Schirmer, Inc.
    No. 3. Despairing, cursing rage — Last 7 bars.

Haydn, Josef, *The Seasons* — G. Schirmer, Inc.
    No. 21. Hark: the deep tremendous voice — Letter F Bars 7-10, 14-21.

Hindemith, Paul, *Apparebit Repentina Dies* — Schott & Co., Ltd.
    Part I. Bars 84-91.

Holst, Gustav, *1st Choral Symphony* — London Novello & Co., Ltd.
    No. IV. Finale — No. 61 Bars 2-12.

Mendelssohn, Felix, *Elijah* — G. Schirmer, Inc.
    No. 11. Baal, we cry to thee — Bar 36 ff.
    No. 13. Baal! Baal! — Bars 5-12.
    No. 34. Behold, God the Lord — Bars 6-9, 41-44, 106-114.
    No. 38. Then did Elijah — Last 4 bars.

Prokofieff, Serge, *Alexander Nevsky* — Leeds Music Corp.
    No. 7. Alexander's Entry in Pskov — Bars 6-10, No. 87 Bars 1-14.

Poulenc, Francis, *Secheresses* — Durand & Co.
    No. I. Les sauterelles — Bars 71-77.

Vaughan Williams, Ralph, *A Sea Symphony* — Stainer and Bell, Ltd.
    No. IV. The explorers — Letter H Bars 11-22, Letter W Bars 1-9.

Flowing Melodic Line

Bantock, Granville, *The Burden of Babylon* — Joseph Williams, Ltd.
    No. 26 Bar 7 ff.

Borodin, Alexander, *Prince Igor* — Boosey & Hawkes, Ltd.
    Choral dance No. 17. Letter P Bars 25-30.

Brahms, Johannes, *Schicksalslied* — H. W. Gray Co., Inc.
    Letter M Bars 10-33.

Brahms, Johannes, *Requiem* — G. Schirmer, Inc.
  No. II. Letter A Bars 1-11, Letter B Bars 12-23.
  No. IV. Letter D Bars 2-12.

Foss, Lukas, *The Prairie* — G. Schirmer, Inc.
  Part II. Dust of men — Bars 88-106.

Hindemith, Paul, *Apparebit Repentina Dies* — Schott & Co. Ltd.
  Part III. Bars 142-149.

Honegger, Arthur, *King David* — E. C. Schirmer Music Co.
  No. 20. Psalm — No. 2 Bars 2-11.

Poulenc, Francis, *Secheresses* — Durand & Co.
  No. I. Les sauterelles — Bars 97-104.

Verdi, Giuseppe, *Requiem* — G. Schirmer, Inc.
  No. 2. Day of anger — Letter G Bars 21-31.
  No. 5. Lamb of God — Bars 14-26.

Vaughan Williams, Ralph, *A Sea Symphony* — Stainer and Bell, Ltd.
  No. III. The waves — Letter L Bars 1-7, Letter Aa Bars 1-6.

Rhythmic Melodic Line

Borodin, Alexander, *Prince Igor* — Boosey & Hawkes, Ltd.
  Choral dance No. 17 — Letter W Bars 1-9.

Handel, George Frederick, *The Messiah* — G. Schirmer, Inc.
  No. 53. Worthy is the Lamb — Letter B Bars 1-7.

Harris, Roy, *Blow The Man Down* — Carl Fischer, Inc.
  Bars 117-125, 174-177, 286-292.

Haydn, Josef, *The Seasons* — G. Schirmer, Inc.
  No. 33. Joyful the liquor flows — Letter D Bars 14-24.

Holst, Gustav, *1st Choral Symphony* — London Novello & Co., Ltd.
  Part III. Scherzo — No. 35 Bars 1 ff., No. 37 Bar 7 ff.

Honegger, Arthur, *King David* — E. C. Schirmer Music Co.
  No. 3. Psalm — Bar 2 ff.

Mendelssohn, Felix, *Elijah* — G. Schirmer, Inc.
  No. 16 The fire descends — Last 6 bars.

Poulenc, Francis, *Secheresses* — Durand & Co.
  No. I. Les sauterelles — Bars 35-38.
  No. III. Le faux avenir — Bars 204-207, 210-214.
  No. IV. Le squelette de la mer — Bars 290-294.

Unison As Recitative

Bantock, Granville, *The Burden Of Babylon* — Joseph Williams, Ltd.
  No. 17 Bars 1-6.

Beethoven, Ludwig von, *Missa Solemnis In D* — G. Schirmer, Inc.
  Et incarnatus — Letter L Bars 1-2.

Holst, Gustav, *1st Choral Symphony* — London Novello & Co., Ltd.
  Prelude — Bar 5 ff.

Stravinsky, Igor, *Symphonie Des Psaumes* — Boosey & Hawkes, Ltd.
  Part III. No. 8 Bars 1-6.

Verdi, Giuseppe, *Requiem* — G. Schirmer, Inc.
  No. 7. Lord, deliver my soul — Last 4 bars.

Melodic Line In High Range

Bartok, Bela, *Four Slovak Folk Songs* — Boosey & Hawkes, Ltd.
  No. I. Bars 58-76.

Beethoven, Ludwig von, *Missa Solemnis In D* — G. Schirmer, Inc.
  Quoniam — Letter Dd Bars 7-13, Letter Qq Bars 1-5.
  Et resurrexit — Letter Z Bars 1-4.

Borodin, Alexander, *Prince Igor* — Boosey & Hawkes, Ltd.
  Choral dance No. 17 — Letter D Bars 32-39.

Brahms, Johannes, *Requiem* — G. Schirmer, Inc.
  No. II. Letter A Bars 12-23, Letter F Bars 1-11.
  No. VI. Letter C Bars 2-7.

Foss, Lukas, *The Prairie* — G. Schirmer, Inc.
  Part II. Dust of men — Bars 209-213.

Prokofieff, Serge, *Alexander Nevsky* — Leeds Music Corp.
  No. 3. The Crusaders in Pskov — No. 17 Bars 1-8.
  No. 5. The battle on ice — No. 48 Bar 2 ff.

Respighi, Ottorino, *La Primavera* — Universal-Edition.
  No. 66 Bars 5-11.

Melodic Line In Alternate Voices

Borodin, Alexander, *Prince Igor* — Boosey & Hawkes, Ltd.
  Choral dance No. 17 — Letter E Bars 1-16.

Harris, Roy, *Blow the Man Down* — Carl Fischer, Inc.
  Bar 16 ff., 59 ff.

Hindemith, Paul, *Apparebit Repentina Dies* — Schott and Co., Ltd.
  Part I. Bars 170-179.
  Part III. Bars 150-157.

Honegger, Arthur, *King David* — E. C. Schirmer Music Co.
  No. 16 The Dance Before the Ark — No. 17 Bars 1-8.

Mendelssohn, Felix *Elijah* — G. Schirmer, Inc.
  No. 11. Baal, we cry to thee — Bar 36 ff.

Poulenc, Francis, *Secheresses* — Durand & Co.
  No. 1. Les sauterelles — Bars 33-38.

Prokofieff, Serge, *Alexander Nevsky* — Leeds Music Corp.
  No. 2. Song about Alexander Nevsky — No. 8 Bars 1-28.

Verdi, Giuseppe, *Requiem* — G. Schirmer, Inc.
    No. 2. Day of anger — Letter E Bars 1-8.

Alternation of Unison with Harmony

Bantock, Granville, *The Burden of Babylon* — Joseph Williams, Ltd.
    No. 39 Bars 1-7.

Beethoven, Ludwig von, *Missa Solemnis In D* — G. Schirmer, Inc.
    Gloria — Letter U Bars 6-11.

Brahms, Johannes, *Requiem* — G. Schirmer, Inc.
    No. VI. Letter C Bars 5-11.

Foss, Lukas, *The Prairie* — G. Schirmer, Inc.
    Part III. They are mine — Bars 284-295.

Handel, George Frederick, *The Messiah* — G. Schirmer, Inc.
    No. 44. Hallelujah — Bars 12-21.

Mendelssohn, Felix, *Elijah* — G. Schirmer, Inc.
    No. 41 But the Lord from the North — Bars 2-8.

Stravinsky, Igor, *Symphonie Des Psaumes* — Boosey & Hawkes, Ltd.
    Part II. No. 14 Bar 1 ff.

Verdi, Giuseppe, *Requiem* —G. Schirmer, Inc.
    No. 2. Day of anger — Bars 3-19.
    No. 4. Holy — Last 8 bars.

Vaughan Williams, Ralph, *A Sea Symphony* — Stainer and Bell, Ltd.
    No. I. A song for all seas, all ships — Letter I Bars 1-4.
    Letter T Bars 10-12, Letter Cc Bars 6-9.
    No. II. On the beach at night alone — Letter L Bar 1 ff.
    No. III. The waves — Letter Dd Bars 3-8.

Traditional Five-Part Writing

Bach, Johann Sebastian, *Jesu, Priceless Treasure* — G. Schirmer, Inc.
    No. 2. So there is now no condemnation — Bar 1 ff.
    No. 3. In Thine arm I rest me — Bar 1 ff.
    No. 5. Death, I do not fear thee — Bar 1 ff.
    No. 10. If by His spirit — Bar 1 ff.

Bach, Johann Sebastian, *Mass In B Minor* — H. W. Gray Co., Inc.
    No. 1. Kyrie eleison — Bars 1-4.

Thompson, Randall, *Five Odes Of Horace* — E. C. Schirmer Music Co.
    O fons bandusiae — Bar 75 ff.

Close Harmonization In Multiple Parts

Bantock, Granville, *The Burden of Babylon* — Joseph Williams, Ltd.
No. 43. Bars 6-8.

Holst, Gustav, *1st Choral Symphony* — London Novello & Co., Ltd.
No. 2. Ode on a Grecian Urn — No. 31 Bars 1-4.

Prokofieff, Serge, *Alexander Nevsky* — Leeds Music Corp.
No. 7. Alexander's Entry in Pskov — No. 91 Bars 1-9.

Poulenc, Francis, *Secheresses* — Durand & Co.
No. I. Les sauterelles — Bars 78-84.
No. III. Le faux avenir — Bars 237-238.

Walton, William, *Belshazzar's Feast* — Oxford University Press.
No. 77 Bars 15-20.

Vaughan Williams, Ralph, *A Sea Symphony* — Stainer and Bell, Ltd.
No. I. A song for all seas, all ships — Letter Cc Bars 7-9.
No. III. The waves — Letter Q Bars 3-6.
No. IV. The explorers — Letter G Bars 15-17.

Wide Spread Multiple Parts

Bantock, Granville, *The Burden of Babylon* — Joseph Williams, Ltd.
No. 6 Bar 9 ff., No. 9 Bars 5-9, No. 35 Bar 5 ff., No. 38 Bar 5 ff.

Delius, Frederic, *Sea Drift* —Boosey & Hawkes, Ltd.
No. 11 Bars 8-11, No. 19 Bars 1-4.

Dello Joio, Norman, *Song Of The Open Road* — Carl Fischer, Inc.
Deciso — Bars 9-15.

Foss, Lukas, *The Prairie* — G. Schirmer, Inc.
Part III. They are mine — Bars 228-230.
Part VI. Cool prayers — Bars 28-35.

Holst, Gustav, *1st Choral Symphony* — London Novello & Co., Ltd.
No. II. Ode on a Grecian urn — No. 25 Bars 1-7.
No. IV. Finale — Bars 6-9.

Mendelssohn, Felix, *Elijah* — G. Schirmer, Inc.
No. 41. But the Lord from the North — Last 5 bars.

Respighi, Ottorino, *La Primavera* — Universal-Edition.
No. 11 Bars 5-9, No. 64 Bars 1-5, 15-20.

Schonberg, Arnold, *Gurre-lieder* — Universal-Edition.
Part III. No. 92 Bars 3-12, No. 99 Last 4 bars.

Verdi, Giuseppe, *Requiem* — G. Schirmer, Inc.
No. 2. Day of anger — Bars 5-9, 15-19.
No. 4. Holy — Bars 6-8, Last 6 bars.

Walton, William, *Belshazzar's Feast* —Oxford University Press.
No. 22 Bars 11-13, No. 24 Bars 1-7, No. 59 Bars 17-19.

Vaughan Williams, Ralph, *A Sea Symphony* — Stainer and Bell, Ltd.
No. IV. The explorers — Letter Bb Bars 16-19.

Figuration Or Counter In One Or More Parts

Bach, Johann Sebastian, *Jesu, Priceless Treasure* — G. Schirmer, Inc.
No. 5. Death, I do not fear thee — Bars 16-19.

Bach, Johann Sebastian, *Mass In B Minor* — H. W. Gray Co., Inc.
No. 20. Sanctus — Bars·1-3, 7-9, 17-22, Letter E Bars 1-6,
Letter N Bars 1-6.
No. 21. Hosannah — Bars 26-28, 30-32, 34-36.

Bantock, Granville, *The Burden of Babylon* — Joseph Williams, Ltd.
No. 6 Bars 3-8, No. 14 Bar 3 ff., No. 19 Bar 1 ff., No. 27 Bars 9-12.
No. 28 Bars 1-3, 7-13, No. 40 Bar 5 ff.

Borodin, Alexander, *Prince Igor* — Boosey & Hawkes, Ltd.
Choral dance No. 17 — Letter P Bars 1-15.

Foss, Lukas, *The Prairie* — G. Schirmer, Inc.
Part III. They are mine — Bars 175-180.

Prokofieff, Serge, *Alexander Nevsky* — Leeds Music Corp.
No. 3. The Crusaders in Pskov — No. 15 Bar 1 ff.

Respighi, Ottorino, *La Primavera* — Universal-Edition.
No. 14 Bars 1-5.

Thompson, Randall, *Five Odes Of Horace* — E. C. Schirmer Music Co.
O Venus regina — Bars 23-33.

Walton, William, *Belshazzar's Feast* — Oxford University Press.
No. 2 Bars 1-5, No. 58 Bars 1-4.

Mixed Voicing

Bantock, Granville, *The Burden of Babylon* — Joseph Williams, Ltd.
No. 17 Bars 9-10, No. 18 Bars 1-5.

Holst, Gustav, *1st Choral Symphony* — London Novello & Co., Ltd.
No. 1. Song and Bacchanal — No. 18 Bar 2 ff.
No. 2 Ode on a Grecian urn — No. 21 Bar 2 ff.

Walton, William, *Belshazzar's Feast* —Oxford University Press.
No. 11 Bars 13-16, No. 12 Bars 1-8.

Vaughan Williams, Ralph, *A Sea Symphony* — Stainer and Bell, Ltd.
No. II. On the beach at night alone — Letter M Bars 5-10.

CHAPTER EIGHT   SPECIAL TECHNIQUES

Chorus As Answer To Solo Voice Or Section

Beethoven, Ludwig von, *Missa Solemnis In D* — G. Schirmer, Inc.
Kyrie — Bars 21-34.
Et resurrexit — Bars 1-6.

Brahms, Johannes, *Requiem* — G. Schirmer, Inc.
    No. III. Letter C Bars 15-28.

Foss, Lukas, *The Prairie* — G. Schirmer, Inc.
    Part II. Dust of men — Bar 162 ff.

Handel, George Frederick, *The Messiah* —G. Schirmer, Inc.
    No. 4. And the glory of the Lord — Bars 11-17.
    No. 33. Lift up your heads — Letter E Bars 3-6.

Haydn, Josef, *The Creation* —G. Schirmer, Inc.
    No. 5. The marv'lous work — Bar 35 ff.

Mendelssohn, Felix, *Elijah* —G. Schirmer, Inc.
    No. 5. Yet doth the Lord — Bars 3-6, 9-12.

Milhaud, Darius, *Miracles Of Faith* — G. Schirmer, Inc.
    Part II. Bars 57-75.

Mozart, Wolfgang Amadeus, *Requiem Mass* — H. W. Gray Co., Inc.
    No. 2. Dies irae — Bars 40-52.

Vaughan Williams, Ralph, *A Sea Symphony* — Stainer and Bell, Ltd.
    No. I. A song for all seas, all ships — Letter L Bar 8 ff.

Solo Voice And Chorus Together

Brahms, Johannes, *Requiem* — G. Schirmer, Inc.
    No. V Letter A Bars 5-10.

Britten, Benjamin, *Hymn To St. Cecilia* — Boosey & Hawkes, Ltd.
    Andante comodo — Bar 22 ff.

Delius, Frederic, *Sea Drift* — Boosey & Hawkes, Ltd.
    No. 19 Bar 8 ff.

Haydn, Josef, *The Creation* — G. Schirmer, Inc.
    No. 5. The marv'lous work — Bars 16-22.

Verdi, Giuseppe, *Requiem* — G. Schirmer. Inc.
    No. 7. Lord, deliver my soul — Letter C Bar 42 ff.

Vaughan Williams, Ralph, *A Sea Symphony* — Stainer and Bell, Ltd.
    No. I. A song for all seas, all ships — Letter U Bar 7 ff.

Harmonic Pedal Point

Bach, Johann Sebastian, *Jesu, Priceless Treasure* — G. Schirmer, Inc.
    Death, I do not fear thee — Bars 11-14, 29-32.

Beethoven, Ludwig von, *Missa Solemnis In D* — G. Schirmer, Inc.
    Et resurrexit — Letter Ll Bars 6-12.

Brahms, Johannes, *Shicksalslied* — H. W. Gray Co., Inc.
    Letter L Bars 21-27.

Mendelssohn, Felix, *Elijah* — G. Schirmer, Inc.
    No. 5. Yet doth the Lord — Bars 59-66.

Verdi, Giuseppe, *Requiem* — G. Schirmer, Inc.
Requiem and Kyrie — Bars 7-9.

Walton, William, *Belshazzar's Feast* — Oxford University Press.
No. 14 Bars 1-11, No. 59 Bars 7-16, No. 72 Bar 6 ff.

Vaughan Williams, Ralph, *A Sea Symphony* — Stainer and Bell, Ltd.
No. I. A song for all seas, all ships — Letter A Bars 4-23.

The Fan

Bach, Johann Sebastian, *Jesu, Priceless Treasure* — G. Schirmer, Inc.
No. 5. Death, I do not fear thee — Letter G Bars 1-4.

Brahms, Johannes, *Schicksalslied* — H. W. Gray Co., Inc.
Letter I Bars 21-30.

Brahms, Johannes, *Requiem* — G. Schirmer, Inc.
No. I. Letter A Bars 5-9.
No VI.. 4th and 5th bars before the end.

Haydn, Josef, *The Creation* — G. Schirmer, Inc.
No. 14. The heavens are telling — Bars 8-10, 14-16.

Haydn, Josef, *The Seasons* — G. Schirmer, Inc.
No. 7. Be Propitious, Bounteous Heaven — Letter B Bars 22-26.
No. 46. Then comes the dawn — Letter G Bars 5-6, 7-8.

Mozart, Wolfgang Amadeus, *Requiem Mass* — H. W. Gray Co., Inc.
No. 4. Rex tremendae — Bars 6-7.

The Pyramid

Beethoven, Ludwig von, *Missa Solemnis In D* — G. Schirmer, Inc.
Qui tollis — Letter Y Bar 1.
Et resurrexit — Letter Qq Bars 1-3.

Brahms, Johannes, *Requiem* — G. Schirmer, Inc.
No. III. Letter F Bars 21-22.

Dello Joio, Norman, *Song Of The Open Road* — Carl Fischer, Inc.
Deciso — Bars 3-8.

Foss, Lukas, *The Prairie* — G. Schirmer, Inc.
Part III. They are mine — Bars 257-260.

Holst, Gustav, *1st Choral Symphony* — London Novello & Co., Ltd.
No. I. Song and Bacchanal — No. 17 Bars 10-12.

Milhaud, Darius, *Miracles Of Faith* — G. Schirmer, Inc.
Introduction — Bars 24-26.

Respighi, Ottorino, *La Primavera* — Universal-Edition.
No. 11 Bars 1-4, No. 45 Bars 3-5.

Vaughan Williams, Ralph, *A Sea Symphony* — Stainer and Bell, Ltd.
No. III. The waves — Letter F Bars 8-11.
No. IV. The explorers — Letter U Bars 1-6.

Verdi, Giuseppe, *Requiem* — G. Schirmer, Inc.
No. 7 Lord, deliver my soul — Letter C Bars 67-70.

Walton, William, *Belshazzar's Feast* — Oxford University Press.
No. 10 Bars 2-8, 10-14.

The Descant

Bantock, Granville, *The Burden Of Babylon* — Joseph Williams, Ltd.
No. 30 Bar 7 ff., No. 32 Bar 3 ff.

McDonald, Harl, *Songs Of Conquest* — Elkan-Vogel Co., Inc.
No. 2. A complaint against the bitterness — Bars 22-29.

Antiphonal Effects

Bach, Johann Sebastian, *Mass In B Minor* — H. W. Gray Co., Inc.
No. 21. Hosannah — Bars 10-12, Letter S Bars 2-5, Letter U Bars 1-5.

Beethoven, Ludwig von, *Missa Solemnis* — G. Schirmer, Inc.
Kyrie — Letter N Bars 1-8.
Quoniam — Letter Ss Bars 1-3, 8-11.

Foss, Lukas, *The Prairie* — G. Schirmer, Inc.
Part III. They are mine — Bars 171-174.

Haydn, Josef, *The Creation* — G. Schirmer, Inc.
No. 11. Awake the harp — Bars 7-9.

Mendelssohn, Felix, *Elijah* — G. Schirmer, Inc.
'No. 5. Yet doth the Lord — Bars 1-4, 7-10.
No. 11. Baal, we cry to thee — Bars 1-8, 16-18, Last 9 bars.
No. 13. Baal, Baal — Bars 1-4.

Poulenc, Francis, *Secheresses* — Durand & Co.
No. 3. Le faux avenir — Bars 259-261.

CHAPTER NINE   CONTRAPUNTAL TECHNIQUES

Countermelody

Bach, Johann Sebastian, *Mass in B Minor* — H. W. Gray., Inc.
No. 13. Patrem omnipotem — Bars 1-8.
No. 20. Sanctus — Bars 1-6.

Bantock, Granville, *The Burden of Babylon* — Joseph Williams, Ltd.
No. 11 Bars 3-10, No. 23 Bar 5 ff., No. 40 Bar 5 ff.

Borodin, Alexander, *Prince Igor* — Boosey & Hawkes, Ltd.
Choral Dance No. 17. Letter O Bars 1-15. Letter P Bars 1-15.

Britten, Benjamin, *Hymn to St. Cecilia* — Boosey & Hawkes, Ltd.
Tranquillo ecomodo — Bars 1-28.

Handel, George Frederick, *The Messiah* — G. Schirmer, Inc.
No. 4. And the Glory of the Lord— Bars 25-28, Letter B Bars 1-12,
Letter D Bars 1-4, Letter F Bars 7-11.

Haydn, Joseph, *The Seasons* — G. Schirmer, Inc.
No. 10. God Light — Letter B Bars 1-5.

Hindemith, Paul, *Apparebit Repentia Dies* — Schott & Co., Ltd.
Part I. Bars 71-82.
Part III. Bars 60-67, 126 ff.

Mendelssohn, Felix, *Elijah* — G. Schirmer, Inc.
No. 13. Baal! Baal! Bars 21-29.

Prokofieff, Serge, *Alexander Nevsky* — Leeds Music Corp.
No. 3. The Crusaders in Pskov — No. 15 Bar 1 ff., No. 21 Bar 1 ff.

Stravinsky, Igor, *Symphonie des Psaumes* — Boosey & Hawkes, Ltd.
Part II. No. 9 Bar 1 ff.
Part III. No. 6 Bars 2-14, No. 11 Bars 1-12.

Thompson, Randall, *Five Odes of Horace* — E. C. Schirmer Music Co.
O fons bandusiae — Bars 5-17.

Verdi, Giuseppe, *Requiem* — G. Schirmer, Inc.
Hark! the trumpet — Bars 3-8.

Walton, William, *Belshazzar's Feast* — Oxford Universtiy Press.
No. 55 Bars 7-16.

Figuration

Bach, Johann Sebastian, *Mass in B Minor* — H. W. Gray Co., Inc.
No. 20. Sanctus — Bars 26-36.

Bantock, Granville, *The Burden of Babylon* — Joseph Williams, Ltd.
No. 14 — Bar 2 ff.

Brahms, Johannes, *Requiem* — G. Schirmer, Inc.
No. II. Letter I Bars 1-4.

Foss, Lukas, *The Prairie* — G. Schirmer, Inc.
Part IV. When the Red and White men met — Bar 39 ff.

Handel, George Frederick, *The Messiah* — G. Schirmer, Inc.
No. 44. Hallelujah — Letter E Bars 8-16.

Haydn, Joseph, *The Seasons* — G. Schirmer, Inc.
No. 21. Hark! the deep tremendous voice — Letter B Bar 6 ff.
No. 27 B. Achiv'd is the glorious work — Bars 9-12.

Honegger, Arthur, *King David* — E. C. Schirmer Music Co.
No. 16. The Dance Before the Ark — No. 10 Bars 4-8.

Thompson, Randall, *Five Odes of Horace* — E. C. Schirmer Music Co.
O Venus regina — Bars 23-33.

Vaughan Williams, Ralph, *A Sea Symphony* — Stainer and Bell, Ltd.
No. 3. The waves — Letter B Bars 9-15.

Verdi, Giuseppe, *Requiem* — G. Schirmer, Inc.
No. 2 Day of anger — Letter A Bars 9-16.

Walton, William, *Belshazzar's Feast* — Oxford University Press.
No. 2 Bars 1-5, No. 74 Bar 1 ff.

Ostinato

Bantock, Granville, *The Burden of Babylon* — Joseph Williams, Ltd.
No. 28 Bars 7-16.

Bartok, Bela, *Four Slovak Folk Songs* — Boosey & Hawkes, Ltd.
No. IV. Bars 1-9.

McDonald, Harl, *Songs of Conquest* — Elkan-Vogel Co., Inc.
No. III A declaration for increase of understanding — Bars 24-36.

Milhaud, Darius, *Miracles of Faith* — G. Schirmer, Inc.
Part 2. Bars 86-96.

Free Counterpoint

Bach, Johann Sebastian, *Mass in B Minor* — H. W. Gray Co., Inc.
No. 16. Crucifixus — Letter A Bar 1 ff.

Britten Benjamin, *Hymn to St. Cecilia* — Boosey & Hawkes, Ltd.
Andante comodo — Bar 1 ff.

Brahms, Johannes, *Requiem* — G. Schirmer Inc.
No I. Letter B Bars 5-14.

Mendelssohn, Felix, *Elijah* — G. Schirmer, Inc.
No. 29. He, watching over Israel — Bars 44-63.

Vaughan Williams, Ralph, *A Sea Symphony* — Stainer and Bell, Ltd.
A song for all seas, all ships — Letter X Bar 4 ff.

Verdi, Giuseppe, *Requiem* — G. Schirmer, Inc.
No. 7. Lord, deliver my soul — Bar 1 ff.

Canonic and Fugal Writing

Bach, Johann Sebastian, *Mass in B Minor* — H. W. Gray Co., Inc.
No. 6 Gratias agimus — Bar 1 ff.
No. 8 Qui tollis — Bar 1 ff.
No. 19. Confiteor unum baptisma — Bars 1 ff.
No. 24. Dona nobis pacem — Bar 1 ff.

Brahms, Johannes, *Requiem* — G. Schirmer, Inc.
No. VI. Allegro — Bar 1 ff.

Delius, Frederick, *Sea Drift* — Boosey & Hawkes, Ltd.
No. 7 Bar 1 ff.

Handel, George Frederick, *The Messiah* — G. Schirmer, Inc.
    No. 21. His yoke is easy — Bar 1 ff.
    No. 55. Worthy is the Lamb — Letter F Bar 1 ff.

Haydn, Josef, *The Creation* — G. Schirmer, Inc.
    No. 33. Sing the Lord, ye voices all — Bar 10 ff.

Hindemith, Paul, *Apparebit Repentina Dies* — Schott & Co., Ltd.
    Part I. Bar 142 ff.

Holst, Gustav, *1st Choral Symphony* — London Novello & Co., Ltd.
    Part III. Scherzo — No. 34 Bar 1 ff, No. 43 Bar 1 ff.
    Part IV. Finale — No. 55 Bar 1 ff.

Honegger, Arthur, *King David* — E. C. Schirmer Music Co.
    No. II. Psalm — Bar 17 ff.
    No. 19. Psalm of penitence — Bar 2 ff.
    No. 20. Psalm — No. 3 Bar 1 ff.

Mendelssohn, Felix, *Elijah* — G. Schirmer, Inc.
    No. 5. Yet doth the Lord — Bar 18 ff.
    No. 12. Hear our cry, O Baal! — Bar 3 ff.

Mozart, Wolfgang Amadeus, *Requiem Mass* — H. W. Gray Co., Inc.
    No. 6. Confutatis maledictis — Bars 1-6.

Respighi, Ottorino, *La Primavera* — Universal-Edition.
    No. 35 Bar 1 ff.

Schonberg, Arnold, *Gurre-lieder* — Universal-Edition.
    No. 96 Bar 2 ff.

Stravinsky, Igor, *Symphonie des Psaumes* — Boosey & Hawkes, Ltd.
    Part II. No. 5 Bar 1 ff.
    Part III. No. 20 Bar 1 ff.

Vaughan Williams, Ralph, *A Sea Symphony* — Stainer and Bell, Ltd.
    No. 1. A Song for all seas, all ships — Bars 8-16, Letter Z Bar 11 ff.

CHAPTER TEN   SPECIAL MIXED VOICE GROUPINGS

SAB Writing

Buccherini, Luigi, *Stabat Mater fur 3 Singstimmen* — Breitkopf & Hartel.
Cherubini, Luigi, *Offertorium zur Oten Messe* — A. Diabelli & Co.
Cross, Henry B., *Washington* — J. Fischer & Bro.
Hindemith, Paul, *Lieder fur Sing Kriese* — B. Schott's Sohne.
Indy, Vincent d', *Cantate Domino* — A. Durand & fils.
Methfessel, Albert, *Es tonen die Horner* — F. Hofmeister.
Ratez, Emil, *La derniere halte* — J. Hamelle.
Ringwald,Roy, *Praise Him* — Shawnee Press.
Schaller, Artur, *Ei du feiner Reiter* — Kistner & Siegel.

Simeone, Harry, *Youth Sings* — Shawnee Press.
Sowerby, Leo, *The Snow Lay on the Ground* — The H. W. Gray Co., Inc.

SB Writing

See Bibliography of Supplementary Examples for SA Writing. pp. 219-220

CHAPTER ELEVEN   TREBLE VOICE CHORUSES

SSA Writing

Bantock, Granville, *Elfen-Musik* — Breitkopf & Hartel.
Brahms, Johannes, *Part Songs for Female Voices* — J. Church & Co.,
Copland, Aaron, *An Immorality* — E. C. Schirmer Music Co.
Debussy, Claude, *Salut Printemps* — Choudens.
Hindemith, Paul, *Lied von der Musik* — B. Schott's Sohne.
Hindemith, Paul, *Chorlieder fur Knaben* — B. Schott's Sohne.
Hoffman, Albert, *Kommt sum Tanz* — C. F. Vieweg.
Hoffman, Heinrich, *Song of the Norns* — G. Schirmer, Inc.
Ibert, Jacques, *Deux chantes de carnaval de Machiavel* — Heugel et Cie.
Indy, Vincent d', *Sur la mer* — J. Hamelle.
Mendelssohn, Felix, *Elijah* — G. Schirmer, Inc.
     No. 28. Lift thine eyes. Bar 1 ff.
Schumann, Robert, *Zigeunerleben* — Breitkopf & Hartel.
Thompson, Randall, *Rosemary* — E. C. Schirmer Music Co.
Tschaikowsky, Peter, *Natur und Liebe* — D. Rahter.

SSAA Writing

Brahms, Johannes, *12 Lieder und Romanzen fur Frauenchor* — C. F. Peters.
Chausson, Ernest, *Chant Funebre* — Edition Mutuelle.
Giannini, Vittorio, *Lament for Adonis* — G. Ricordi.
Grieg, Edvard, *Vor der Klosterpforte* — C. F. Peters.
Loeffler, Charles, *Evocation* — C. C. Birchard.
Parker, Horatio, *Seven Greek pastoral scenes* – G. Schirmer, Inc.
Saint-Saens, Camille, *La Nuit* — A. Durand.
Schumann, Robert, *Frauenchore* — Universal-Edition.
Thompson, Randall, *Rosemary* — E. C. Schirmer Music Co.
Vaughan Williams, Ralph, *Five Tudor Portraits* — Oxford University Press.

SA Writing

Abt, Franz, *Songs of Woodland and Field* — Augener and Co.
Cowell, Henry, Three two-part songs for women's voices — Music Press, Inc.
Delibes, Leo, *Quinze meodies et deux choeurs* — Heugel et Cie.
Franck, Cesar, *Six duos pour voix egales* — Enoch et Cie.
Gliere, Reinhold, *Suite fur zwei — stimmingen Frauenchor* — P. Jurgenson.

Hadley, Henry, *The Fairy Wedding* — C. C. Birchard.

Massenet, Jules, *Scenes chorales pour deux voix de femmes* — Heugel et Cie.

Rachmaninoff, Sergei, *Six choruses for two-part women's voices* —
Boston Music Co.

CHAPTER TWELVE   MALE CHORUSES

TTBB Writing

Brahms, Johannes, *Fünf Lieder für Männerchor* — C. F. Peters.

Debussy, Claude, *Invocation* — Choudens.

Foss, Lukas, *The Prairie* — G. Schirmer, Inc.
No. II. Dust of men — Bars 319-331.

Franz, Robert, *Sechs Lieder für vierstimmigen Männerchor* — C. F. Peters.

Mendelssohn, Felix, *Elijah* — G. Schirmer, Inc.
No. 11. Baal, we cry to thee. Bars 1-4, 8-12, 25-27.

Mendelssohn, Felix, *Festegesang an die Künstler* — N. Simrock.

Parker, Horatio, *The Norsemen's Raid* — The John Church Co.

Poulenc, Francis, *Chanson a Boire* — Rouart, Lerolle.

Schubert, Franz, *Saemtliche Männerchore* — Universal — Edition.

Schumann, Robert, *Das Glück von Edenhall* — J. Rieter-Biedermann.

Strauss, Richard, *Die Tageszeiten* — F. E. C. Leuckart.

Vaughan Williams, Ralph, *A Sea Symphony* — Stainer & Bell, Ltd.
No. III. The Waves — Letter A Bars 4-8.

Thompson, Randall, *A Testament of Freedom* — E. C. Schirmer Music Co.

Barber Shop Writing

Spaeth, Sigmund, *Barber Shop Ballads* — Prentice-Hall, Inc.

Songs for Men, Books 5,6,7,8 — S.P.E.B.S.Q.S.A.

TTB Writing

Beethoven, Ludwig von, *Bundeslied* — B. Schott & Sohne.

Borodin, Alexander, *Prince Igor* — Boosey & Hawkes, Ltd. —
Letter N Bars 1-16.

Holst, Gustav, *1st Choral Symphony* — London Novello & Co., Ltd.
No. I. Song and Bacchanal — No. 15 Bars 3-9.
No. II. Ode on a Grecian urn — No. 26 Bars 5-8.

McDonald, Harl, *Songs of Conquest* — Elkan-Vogel Co., Inc.
No. IV. The exaltation of man — Bars 3-7, 51-63.

Piston, Walter, *Carnival Song* — Arrow Music Press.

Poulenc, Francis, *Chansons Francaises* — Rouart, Lerolle et Cie.

Respighi, Ottorino, *La Primavera* — Universal-Edition.
No. 8 Bars 11-18.

Thompson, Randall, *Five Odes of Horace* — E. C. Schirmer Music Co.
O Venus Regina — Bars 15-22, 43-46, 50-53.

Vaughan Williams, Ralph, *Five Tudor Portraits* — Oxford University Press.
Walton, William, *Belshazzar's Feast* — Oxford University Press.
  No. 4 Bars 1-9.

TB Writing

Beethoven, Ludwig von, *Missa Solemnis in D* — G. Schirmer, Inc.
  Gloria — Letter U Bars 17-20, 25-26.
  Dona Nobis — Letter I Bars 1-4.
Bruch, Max, *Normannenzug* — Breitkopf & Hartel.
Handel, George Frederick, *The Messiah* — G. Schirmer, Inc.
  No. 33. Lift Up Your Heads — Letter A Bars 1-5.
Haydn, Josef, *The Seasons* — G. Schirmer, Inc.
  No. 9 Spring, her lovely charms unfolding — Letter D Bars 9-13.
  No. 31. Hark! the mountains resound — Letter A Bars 2-9, Letter C
  Bars 14-20.
  No. 33. Joyful the liquor flows — Letter C Bars 2-6, Letter E
  Bars 2-12, Bar 17 ff.

Honegger, Arthur, *King David* — London Novello & Co., Inc.
  No. 8. Song of the prophets — Bars 1-5.
Mozart, Wolfgang Amadeus, *Requiem Mass* — H. W. Gray Co., Ltd.
  No. 6. Confutatis maledictis — Bars 1-6, 11-16.
Respighi, Ottorino, *La Primavera* Universal-Edition.
  No. 8 Bars 7-10.
Strauss, Richard, *Austria* — E. Bote & G. Beck.
Stravinsky, Igor, *Symphonie des Psaumes* — Boosey & Hawkes, Ltd.
  Part II. No. 9 Bar 1 ff.

CHAPTER FOURTEEN   INTRODUCTIONS AND ENDINGS

Introduction Drawn From Thematic Material

Bach, Johann Sebastian, *Mass In B Minor* — H. W. Gray Co., Inc.
  Gloria in excelsis — Bars 1-24.

Handel, George Frederick, *The Messiah* — G. Schirmer, Inc.
  No. 4. And the glory of the Lord — Bars 1-11.
  No. 12. For unto us a child is born — Bars 1-6.
  No. 22. Behold the Lamb of God — Bars 1-4.
  No. 33. Lift up your heads — Bars 1-4.
  No. 44. Hallelujah — Bars 1-3.

Haydn, Josef, *The Creation* — G. Schirmer, Inc.
  No. 3. Now vanish before Thy holy beams — Bars 1-16.
  No. 5. The marv'lous work — Bars 1-4.
  No. 29. (continued) — Of stars the fairest — Bars 1-6.

Haydn, Josef, *The Seasons* — G. Schirmer, Inc.
No. 3. Come, gentle Spring — Bars 1-4.
No. 22. Now cease the conflicts — Bars 1-4.
No. 40. Let the wheel move gaily — Bars 1-4.
No. 42. A wealthy lord, who long hath loved — Bars 1-4.

Mozart, Wolfgang Amadeus, *Requiem Mass* — H. W. Gray Co., Inc.
No. 1. Requiem aeternam — Bars 1-7.
No. 3. Tuba mirum — Bars 1-2.

Introduction Drawn From Figuration or Effect

Bach, Johann Sebastian, *Mass In B Minor* — H. W. Gray Co., Inc.
Crucifixus — Bars 1-4.

Bartok, Bela, *Four Slovak Folk Songs* — Boosey & Hawkes, Ltd.
No. III. Bars 1-4.

Beethoven, Ludwig von, *Missa Solemnis In D* — G. Schirmer, Inc.
Sanctus — Bars 1-11.

Brahms, Johannes, *Requiem* — G. Schirmer, Inc.
No. II. Bars 1-22. No. VII. Bar 1.

Handel, George Frederick, *The Messiah* — G. Schirmer, Inc.
No. 24. Surely He hath borne our griefs — Bars 1-5.

Haydn, Josef, *The Seasons* — G. Schirmer, Inc.
No. 25. Thus Nature ever kind — Bars 1-4.
No. 33. Joyful the liquor flows — Bars 1-3.

Honegger, Arthur, *King David* — E. C. Schirmer Music Co.
No. 24. Psalm — Bar 1.
No 25. Psalm — Bars 1-2.

Milhaud, Darius, *Miracles Of Faith* — G. Schirmer, Inc.
Part I. Daniel and Nebuchadnezzar — Bars 1-4.

Mozart, Wolfgang Amadeus, *Requiem Mass* — H. W. Gray Co., Inc.
No. 4. Rex tremendae — Bars 1-2.
No. 7. Lachrymosa — Bars 1-2.
No. 12. Agnus dei — Bar 1.

Original Material Setting Mood

Bartok, Bela, *Four Slovak Folk Songs* — Boosey & Hawkes, Ltd.
No. I Bars 1-8.

Beethoven, Ludwig von, *Missa Solemnis In D* — G. Schirmer, Inc.
Kyrie — Bars 1-20.
Agnus dei — Bars 1-4.

Haydn, Josef, *The Creation* — G. Schirmer, Inc.
No. 29. By Thee with bliss — Bars 1-4.

Haydn, Josef, *The Seasons* — G. Schirmer, Inc.
 No. 14. Behold, on high He mounts — Bars 1-9.

Honegger, Arthur, *King David* — E. C. Schirmer Music Co.
 No. 20. Psalm — Bars 1-6.

Prokofieff, Serge, *Alexander Nevsky* — Leeds Music Corp.
 No. 2. Song about Alexander Nevsky — Bars 1-8.
 No. 3. The crusaders in Pskov — Bars 1-12.
 No. 4. Arise, ye Russian people — Bars 1-5.
 No. 6. Field of the dead — Bars 1-10.

Verdi, Giuseppe, *Requiem* — G. Schirmer, Inc.
 Requiem and kyrie — Bars 1-6.

Call To Attention

Beethoven, Ludwig von, *Missa Solemnis In D* — G. Schirmer, Inc.
 Gloria — Bars 1-4.
 Credo — Bars 1-4.

Haydn, Joseph, *The Seasons* — G. Schirmer, Inc.
 No. 10. God of light — Bars 1-2.
 No. 21. Hark! The deep tremendous voice — Bars 1-2.

Honegger, Arthur, *King David* — E. C. Schirmer Music Co.
 No. 17. Song — Bars 1-2.

Milhaud, Darius, *Miracles Of Faith* — G. Schirmer, Inc.
 Introduction — Bar 1.

Vaughan Williams, Ralph, *A Sea Symphony* — Stainer and Bell, Ltd.
 No. I. A song for all seas — Bars 1-6.

Verdi, Giuseppe, *Requiem* — G. Schirmer, Inc.
 Day of anger — Bars 1-3.

Extremely Short Introductions

Brahms, Johannes, *Requiem* — G. Schirmer, Inc.
 No. III. — Bar 1.
 No. VI. — Bars 1-2.
 No. VII. — Bar 1.

Handel, George Frederick, *The Messiah* — G. Schirmer, Inc.
 No. 7. He shall purify — Bar 1.

Haydn, Josef, *The Creation* — G. Schirmer, Inc.
 No. 27. Achieved is the glorious work — Bar 1.

Haydn, Josef, *The Seasons* — G. Schirmer, Inc.
 No. 7. Be propitious, bounteous Heaven — Bars 1-2.
 No. 9. Spring, her lovely charms unfolding — Bar 1.

Honegger, Arthur, *King David* — E. C. Schirmer Music Co.
    No. 3. Psalm — Bar 1.
    No. 4. Song of Victory — Bars 1-2.
    No. 11. God, the Lord shall be my light — Bar 1.

Mozart, Wolfgang Amadeus, *Requiem Mass* — H. W. Gray Co., Inc.
    No. 9. Hostias — Bars 1-2.
    No 12. Agnus dei — Bar 1.

Vaughan Williams, Ralph, *A Sea Symphony* — Stainer and Bell, Ltd.
    No. III. The waves — Bars 1-3.

Index

S.P.E.B.S.Q.S.A. (Society for the Preservation and Encouragement of
    Barber Shop Quartet Singing in America), 133
Spacing of voices, 3
Special effects in accompaniments, 39, 196
Special mixed voice groupings, 110-114
Special techniques, 82-96
S.S.A.(A.) writing, 45-52, 115-125; *see* Part writing, Treble voices
Staccato, 185
"Stagger breathing," 183
Staging vocal groups, 174-175
Strings, use of, 186-208
Subdominant, 140
Sustained accompaniments, 35, 82, 189
Swing tunes
    accompaniment, 27, 28
    harmonizations, 23, 78, 79, 121, 122
    in three-part writing, 119
    in traditional four-part writing, 19, 20
"Swipes," 133
Symbols, music; *see* Notation

T.B. writing, 53-59, 137
T.B.B. and T.T.B. writing, 45-52, 134-137
    assignment of melody, 135
    contrapuntal devices, 137
Television, writing for, 175
Tempo changes, 148-150
Text considerations, 99, 102-103
Text-painting, 177, 187, 197
Theater, writing for, 175
Three-part writing, 45-52
    accompanied, 46-48
    in parallel motion, 48
    unaccompanied, 45, 46
    see S.A.B., S.S.A. and T.B.B. writing
Timbre, 4
Tonal tendencies, 8
Tone color, 17-19, 63, 140
Traditional (part) writing, 1-13, 15-20, 45-48, 53-56
    for male voices, 126-132
    in popular ballads and swing tunes, 19
Treble chorus writing
    S.A., 122, 123
    S.S.A., 115-120
    S.S.A.A., 120-122
Treble voices, 46, 48, 51
    with instruments, 187
Trumpets, use of, 208